SQL Server Tuning Scripts
Performance Optimization Secrets

Robin Schumacher

I dedicate this book to Jesus Christ, who chose me to know Him even though I have nothing to offer, my wife Laura, who is the love of my life, and my daughters, Hannah and Claire, who are two of the most beautiful creations ever made by God.

- Robin Schumacher

SQL Server Tuning Scripts
Performance Optimization Secrets

By Robin Schumacher

Copyright © 2014 by Rampant TechPress. All rights reserved.

Printed in the United States of America.

Published by: Rampant TechPress, Kittrell, North Carolina, USA

Editors: Robin Haden and Cindy Cairns

Production Manager: Robert Tuttle

Production Editor: Teri Wade

Cover Design: Bryan Hoff

Illustrations: Mike Reed

Printing History: May 2005, 2014 for First Edition

ISBN: 0-9916386-7-0
ISBN 13: 978-0-9916386-7-3

Library of Congress Control Number: 2014940742

Table of Contents

Table of Contents

Using the Online Code Depot

Purchase of this book provides complete access to the online code depot that contains the sample code scripts. All of the code depot scripts in this book are located at the following URL:

rampant.cc/hpsdba

All of the code scripts in this book are available for download in zip format, ready to load and use. If technical assistance is needed with downloading or accessing the scripts, please contact Rampant TechPress at rtp@rampant.cc.

Are you ready to tune?

ION for Oracle is the premier Oracle tuning tool. ION provides unparalleled capability for time-series Oracle tuning, unavailable anywhere else.

ION can quickly find and plot performance signatures allowing you to see hidden trends, fast. ION interfaces with STATSPACK or AWR to provide unprecedented proactive tuning insights.

Get Ion for Oracle now!

www.ion-dba.com

Oracle Script Collection

Packed with over 600 ready-to-use Oracle scripts, this is the definitive collection for every Oracle professional DBA. It would take many years to develop these scripts from scratch, making this download the best value in the Oracle industry.

It's only $79.95.

For purchase and download go to: www.oracle-script.com or call 800-766-1884.

Conventions Used in this Book

It is critical for any technical publication to follow rigorous standards and employ consistent punctuation conventions to make the text easy to read.

However, this is not an easy task. Within Oracle there are many types of notation that can confuse a reader. Some Oracle utilities such as STATSPACK and TKPROF are always spelled in CAPITAL letters, while Oracle parameters and procedures have varying naming conventions in the Oracle documentation. It is also important to remember that many Oracle commands are case sensitive, and are always left in their original executable form, and never altered with italics or capitalization.

Hence, all Rampant TechPress books follow these conventions:

Parameters - All Oracle parameters will be lowercase italics. Exceptions to this rule are parameter arguments that are commonly capitalized (KEEP pool, TKPROF), these will be left in ALL CAPS.

Variables – All PL/SQL program variables and arguments will also remain in lowercase italics (*dbms_job*, *dbms_utility*).

Tables & dictionary objects – All data dictionary objects are referenced in lowercase italics (*dba_index*es, *v$sql*). This includes all *v$* and *x$* views (*x$kcbcbh*, *v$parameter*) and dictionary views (*dba_tables*, *user_indexes*).

SQL – All SQL is formatted for easy use in the code depote. The main SQL terms (select, from, where, group by, order by, having) will always appear on a separate line.

Programs & Products – All products and programs that are known to the author are capitalized according to the vendor specifications (IBM, DBXray, etc). All names known by Rampant TechPress to be trademark names appear in this text as initial caps. References to UNIX are always made in uppercase.

Acknowledgements

This type of reference book requires the dedicated efforts of many people. I need to thank and acknowledge everyone who helped bring this book to life:

Tom Sager, for graciously taking the time to technically review this book, validate all code examples, and provide excellent insight and expert technical content in the areas of capacity planning and SQL Server optimization.

Don Burleson, for his ever-present enthusiasm and encouragement, which results in making things happen.

Robert Tuttle, for the production management, including the coordination of the cover art, page proofing, printing, and distribution.

Robin Haden and Cindy Cairns for their excellent copy editing.

Teri Wade, for her help in the production of the page proofs.

Bryan Hoff, for his exceptional cover design and graphics.

Janet Burleson, for her assistance with the web site, and for creating the code depot and the online shopping cart for this book.

Linda Webb, for her expert page-proofing services.

With my sincerest thanks,

Robin Schumacher

Preface

My introduction to databases occurred back in 1988, when I started my information technology career at Electronic Data Systems (EDS). Back then, the mainframe ruled as it still does to some degree today, and the relational engine was just beginning to kick up steam. I cut my teeth on version 2.1 of DB2 OS/390 and immediately fell in love with the simplicity and power of storing data in a relational model. I liked the fact that if you could understand a basic table structure of rows and columns, you could get the basics how a RDBMS works.

After a couple of years, I moved from mainframe DB2 to Teradata and then to Oracle. Oracle was my first experience with a client/server or distributed database management system, and I can certainly say that the software produced by the folks at Redwood Shores worked me over pretty well for the first few years. I definitely had a learning curve going from DB2 and Teradata to Oracle, but I survived and still use Oracle quite extensively in my current career. I feel it is one of the most powerful, flexible, and rich RDBMS engines in the world today.

Then one day, someone at a hospital chain I was working for said that they were going to use a database from Microsoft for a particular application instead of Oracle. Being the only DBA, I was handed the administrator manual for Microsoft SQL Server version 4.2. I remember being quite eager to get into the book because I loved (and still do) learning new things. It did not take long to get the concepts of SQL Server down. Coming from the complex world of Oracle, I found a lot of things in SQL Server appealing. I still remember the first time I created a SQL Server database with the first iteration of Microsoft supplied database administration tools. Within a minute or two, I had a new SQL Server database all ready to go. I could not believe it! With Oracle, there were complex database creation scripts to run, manual builds of the data dictionary, and other miscellaneous things to do that took quite a while to complete. This was before the advent of the much improved Oracle Installer, Oracle Enterprise Manager, and other third party database tools. Without a doubt, this new SQL Server RDBMS and I were off to a beautiful start.

Of course, nothing stays that easy. I had to get the hang of Transact-SQL instead of PL/SQL, but that didn't take too long either. If I am pressed to admit which procedural language I'd rather work in, T-SQL will win out over PL/SQL or DB2's procedural language any day. Backup and recovery in SQL Server was a snap compared to other database engines I had worked with, and stopping and starting SQL Server was a cakewalk. Yessir, the Microsoft database was certainly OK in my book.

When I built my first production SQL Server back in the middle 1990's, Microsoft's database was not taken too seriously as a major contender to RDBMS's like Oracle and DB2. But my, how things have changed.

The Momentum and Transformation of SQL Server

Although some may still view SQL Server as a departmental-only solution, the vast majority of the IT world has changed their mind regarding Microsoft's database, and it shows. According to a 2004 Gartner Group database market share study, Microsoft's database growth rate for 2003 eclipsed that of Oracle and IBM by a sizable margin. In 2003, Microsoft SQL Server grew 11 percent to $1.3 billion and increased its market share to 18.7 percent compared to 17.7 percent in the previous year. Oracle's database sales rose a mere 2.4 percent with its market share actually declining to 32.6 percent from 33.4 percent in 2002. IBM's market share remained flat at 35.7 percent, while its database sales saw a 4.9 percent growth rate in 2003.

Not only is Microsoft SQL Server growing in terms of market share and revenue, but Redmond is seeing its database grow in terms of scale and visibility as well. Recent studies put out by the Winter Group confirm this fact. According to Winter's 2003 Top Ten survey, SQL Server databases run the world's second largest workload for transaction processing across all platforms, coming in second only to a large mainframe CA-Datacom system. In fact, SQL Server holds spots two through seven in Winter's OLTP category. In terms of sheer database size, Microsoft cracked the top ten in Winter's survey in 2003 with a number six ranking among all platforms in the OLTP category with Verizon's 5.3 Terabyte transaction processing system. Indeed, all indications point to Microsoft SQL Server being ready, willing, and able to handle high visibility and large-scale projects.

In my job, I get to meet with many industry analysts and speak with them about where the database industry is heading. During a meeting with several well-known analysts at my corporate headquarters, I asked them point blank what database vendor corporations were swapping their existing DBMS vendors out for. Their unanimous response – "Microsoft!" Even with open source databases like MySQL gaining ground and garnering a lot of press, the Microsoft SQL Server machine continues to march upward. In a recent poll (2005) that I conducted of Embarcadero Technologies' 70,000+ customer base, I asked which database platforms our customers were adding and removing. Microsoft came in a strong number two behind Oracle, with virtually no customer site saying they were dropping SQL Server from production use.

While the momentum of SQL Server is good news for Microsoft, it also means that Redmond's database engine is evolving from a behind-the-scenes player to one that is oftentimes alone on center stage in the very bright limelight. Whereas a SQL Server database used to support at most tens of users, SQL Server applications are now being rolled out that serve hundreds or thousands of users. In the same way, the SQL Server systems of yesteryear may have been 100MB or so in size, but now it is not uncommon to read of Microsoft databases that are hundreds of gigabytes in size.

Make no mistake - such elevations in visibility and scope are all that are needed to expose the performance weaknesses of a database's framework. Microsoft SQL Server enjoys a reputation as being an easy to use and somewhat turnkey solution for database applications, with performance management concerns being nonexistent. Much of this reputation has been forged from its vendor-supplied toolset, which helps to visually manage many of the intricacies of the server engine. However, in my opinion, some of this reputation also comes from the uncomplicated departmental systems that SQL Server began life with.

Simply put, any DBMS will appear easy to manage and can perform well when it has a tiny user community and is small in size. But, take that same underlying structure (tables, indexes, etc.), throw thousands of users at it, have it grow exponentially in size, and see if performance problems don't begin to crack the system at its seams. In other words, many DBAs are now waking up to the fact that serious SQL Server databases require every bit as much attention as heavy-duty Oracle, DB2, and Sybase servers.

"But SQL Server is Easy to Use!"

So go the cries of the Microsoft, and every database vendor's, marketing machine. In some ways, yes, SQL Server is quite easy to use as I have already mentioned above. But in other ways, SQL Server is no piece of cake. This is especially true when it comes to performance management and monitoring.

Remember how I mentioned starting my SQL Server love affair at a hospital chain? Well, soon it became time for me to start monitoring the performance and space usage of my new databases. Being accustomed to using a treasure trove of scripts for Oracle monitoring, I began listing what I would need for SQL Server. I clearly remember the day that I started building my first script to monitor space usage for SQL Server. All the docs pointed to the *sp_spaceused* stored procedure as what I needed for monitoring the space for SQL Server. Thinking it would give me what I was looking for, I executed the procedure and saw output similar to this:

database_name	database_size	unallocated space
RMS1	3.94 MB	0.99 MB

reserved	data	index_size	unused
3016 KB	1168 KB	1528 KB	320 KB

I looked at the output, cocked my head, and thought "What the heck is that?!?" I knew the actual database was much bigger than what was listed, so why was the reported database size so much smaller? Where was the amount for the transaction log? In Oracle and other database engines, I was used to very clean data dictionary views that gave me everything I wanted in a clean and easy SQL query. The output for SQL Server's most commonly used space procedure was not at all what I needed or hoped for.

I figured I just needed to dive into the data dictionary, where I knew wonderful views and easy-to-understand data dictionary tables would be waiting for me. After all, SQL Server is easy to use and understand right?

What I found caused me no end of frustration. So, just where were the space amounts for databases? I looked in the *master* database and found the *sysdatabases* table. No luck there. There was a *sysdevices* table, remember this was version 4.2, but all I found there were names of the devices and numeric sizes that did not match how big I knew each device was. Maybe you have to total up the sizes of all the objects, I thought. So I went to *sysobjects*. Nothing. I saw a *sysindexes* table but not a *systables* table. I really rolled my eyes when I found out that SQL Server maintained both index data and table data in the *sysindexes* table!

To be fair to Microsoft, these data dictionary structures were inherited from Sybase, which can be a difficult engine to write diagnostic queries against. Just ask me how I know!! The Redmond database warriors have introduced many new performance views and tables in SQL Server 2005, so things have gotten a lot better in Microsoft's latest revision of their database engine. However, the bottom line is that SQL Server can be just as challenging to dig into as any other RDBMS, so the sooner you come to that realization, the better prepared you will be to manage it.

A Better Approach to Performance Management

Even if you are a seasoned SQL Server professional who is accustomed to digging into the data dictionary to get what you need with scripts and stored procedures, you either have reached the point of understanding that more is needed to intelligently manage the performance of your growing SQL Server farm or you will soon. I say this for a couple of reasons.

First, SQL Server's perceived ease of use can actually backfire on you if you are not careful. Since it's easy to create SQL Server databases, it is not uncommon for a DBA to be shocked at how fast the actual number of databases mushrooms on the servers they manage. Each of these precious creations comes with its own baggage such as backup and recovery responsibilities, storage implications, and so on. Before you know it, you're spiraling out of control with management and performance issues that you never thought you would face.

Second, there is an alarming trend of IT managers who are discounting the need for professional database management. These folks are buying into the marketing machines of the database giants who are trumpeting the supposed "self management" or "self healing" components of their software. I will be the first to say that things have definitely improved in the areas of automation and intelligent self-management of the database engines, but in no way has it eliminated the need for knowledgeable database administrators who oversee the construction and management of critical databases. If anything, the role of the DBA is expanding, becoming more visible, and taking on more responsibility. However, as this occurs, IT management has not become convinced of the need for extra DBA headcount, with the end result being DBAs who are managing many more servers plus extra functions like extract-tranform-load (ETL) operations.

These trends absolutely mandate that the DBA institute a structured plan and methodology for performance management that can scale to hundreds of servers if need be and (gasp!) be extended to handle cross-platform needs that are outside of the SQL Server engine to include the likes of Oracle, IBM, Sybase, MySQL, and others.

What This Book Is and Isn't

Performance Management is what this book is all about. The goal is to help you, the SQL Server professional, establish a rock solid performance strategy that covers all your key database servers and puts you in the driver's seat of control. Yes, there will be plenty of technical discussion with lots of T-SQL queries and procedures you can take and immediately put to use in your environment. But we will spend some up front time introducing the concepts of data lifecycle management, with special emphasis on the area of performance lifecycle management (PLM). We will dive into each phase of PLM to see how you can become more productive than you ever thought possible in the area of managing, and more importantly, ensuring the success and performance of the database systems under your care.

That said, the following are some things this book is not:

- This book is not intended to be thousands of pages in length and able to serve as a huge doorstop. Instead, it's intended to be something that can be read quickly with lots of practical information being taken away and immediately put to use.

- This book will not show a bunch of Enterprise Manager or SQL Workbench pictures, nor will it go through step-by-step instructions of how to run a query through Query Analyzer. I take for granted that you know the in's and out's of how to use Microsoft's supplied tools and have a working knowledge of basic SQL Server architecture.

- This book does not contain a lot of theory, but instead is very 'to the point' with many real world examples being showcased to help you learn what to do, and maybe more importantly, what not to do when working to optimize the performance of your SQL Server systems.

The ultimate responsibility of the database administrator is to safeguard the data assets of the business entity for which they work. A large part of that responsibility revolves around ensuring that critical databases are up and optimized so that key business functions can be carried out in the shortest amount of time possible. It is my hope that you can take the ideas contained in this book and make that goal your reality.

Code Depot User ID = reader, Password = speed

Data Lifecycle Management

Introduction

One thing that many in the database industry agree upon is that the role of the database administrator is changing. While there are some who believe that the DBA's job will become obsolete, the majority of professionals in the industry agree that nothing could be further from the truth.

Indeed, one can make rounds amongst thousands of customers who are utilizing a company's database software tools and actually see that DBAs are now taking a more elevated and visible role than they have in the past. This is exciting!

Seasoned DBAs that spent many years tucked inside a production data center with little outside contact other than phone and email think it is fantastic to see today's DBAs out in front of corporate business customers and overseeing the construction of complex data-driven systems. It is a part of a natural progression for the DBA as the chief protector and lord of corporate data.

This being the case, the first step in the pursuit of becoming a high performance SQL Server DBA is to recognize the fact that the administrator role is likely to grow and encompass much more than babysitting backups and adding user accounts.

In the coming years, DBAs will likely find themselves front and center in activities that range from massive Extract-Transform-Load (ETL) operations to highly visible security activities such as data auditing, which is necessary to comply with Sarbanes Oxley, HIPAA, and other governmental regulations.

The bad news is these are added responsibilities. DBAs will still have to manage all the standard functions that were handled in the past, as well as their new duties. Many DBAs have already experienced this reality.

So what can be done? How can the DBA possibly take care of a growing database server farm and oversee other highly visible data-related activities that will, without question, require a lot of time and attention, and do it all very well? The answer is that today's DBA must become very tuned in to an ideology called Data Lifecycle Management (DLM).

This chapter will cover DLM, with special focus on one of DLM's sub-components called Performance Lifecycle Management. To be successful as a SQL Server DBA, both now and in the future, mastering the concepts of DLM, especially the parts that relate to performance management must be accomplished.

What is Data Lifecycle Management?

DLM is the process of cost-effectively managing and optimizing critical data and database infrastructures. The bottom line is that DLM manages data from its logical conception down to its eventual archival or removal. The three primary components, or layers, of DLM are:

- Data Management Service Layer.
- Database Management Service Layer.
- Performance Management Service Layer.

There is a lot of industry buzz around the concept of DLM. Storage vendors have put their own spin on DLM and coined the phrase,

Information Lifecycle Management (ILM). However, upon closer inspection, ILM is very storage-centric in its definition and management. The ILM vendors do not believe data can be defined until it hits the disk, which naturally upsets many data modelers and data architects.

DLM is similar to ILM in some ways, but it is much more encompassing. Figure 1.1 graphically depicts DLM. Non-relational data sources must be included under the umbrella of DLM, as there is much data managed outside of relational engines like SQL Server.

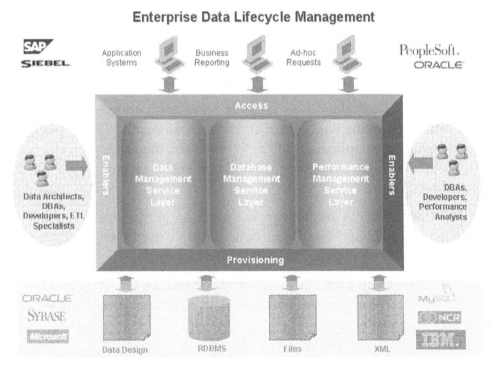

Figure 1.1: *Graphical depiction of data lifecycle management.*

The following sections will present a brief overview of the data and database management service layers, and will then focus on the performance management service layer, which is the central theme of this book. The information on the management layer will reveal how it can be used to help ensure success as a high performance SQL Server DBA.

Data Management

Data management focuses on two primary domains:

- Logical Data Management.
- Physical Data Management.

Logical Data Management, depicted in Figure 1.2, focuses on the following key activities:

Data Definition: This activity involves the logical definition of data. It does not involve the specific assignment of a data model to a particular database engine like SQL Server.

Standards Control: This activity revolves around ensuring data definitions adhere to certain datatype assignments. This can have an impact on performance when, for example, the DBA performs a table join on keys that have been mistakenly created with different datatypes.

Documentation: This activity is based on the premise that all data models and database/object definitions should be easily documented in a variety of formats (HTML, MS Word, etc.)

Metadata Management: This activity concerns the retention and reuse of attribute and datatype definitions, most often in a data dictionary or other repository.

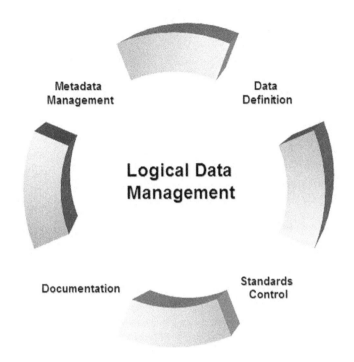

Metadata
Management

Data
Definition

**Logical Data
Management**

Documentation

Standards
Control

Figure 1.2: *The cyclical nature of logical data management.*

Physical Data Management, shown in Figure 1.3 may be something that more SQL Server DBAs are accustomed to carrying out than Logical Data Management.

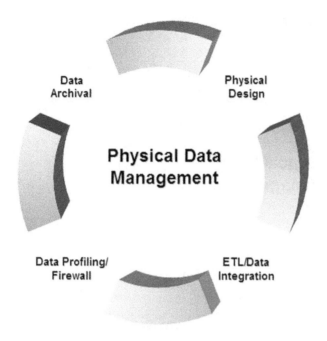

Figure 1.3: *The cyclical nature of physical data management.*

Physical Data Management involves physical design, which will be explained in upcoming chapters. This is perhaps the single most important activity in which the DBA will be involved in that contributes to the overall performance of SQL Server systems.

Another interesting area related to performance in this area of management is data archival. This involves the movement of seldom used data from primary to secondary database servers, and eventually, handles its complete removal. Since corporations are often forced to keep a specified number of years' worth of data online to meet certain government or industry regulations, this function has grown in importance.

The problem is that much of this data is not routinely accessed, so it sits fairly idle in the database. Knowing that it is much faster to scan 10,000 rows than 10,000,000 rows, the purpose behind archiving is to get that seldom accessed data to a place where it remains online but does not impact standard production performance. There are a few third party software vendors providing products to help with this process, with most people still writing manual SQL Server scripts and DTS operations.

Database Management

Database Management is something with which everyone reading this book is very familiar. As a result, it is likely to be review when the standard database management tasks are identified as follows:

- Installation/Configuration.
- Storage Management.
- Schema Design/Management.
- Security Management.
- Backup/Recovery Management.
- Business Logic Construction/Analysis.
- Change Management.
- Job Management.

Many of these areas will be explained as information on performance management is included throughout this book.

Performance Management

Performance Management, as it pertains to the SQL Server, is about the central focus of the remainder of this book. If the DBA is going to be serious about managing the performance of SQL Server systems, then being intimately acquainted with Performance Lifecycle Management (PLM) is a must. PLM is a process of guaranteeing the best possible performance from database driven systems. As depicted in Figure 1.4, PLM can be broken down into five distinct categories:

- Proactive Action

- Monitoring

- Analysis

- Forecasts

- Tuning

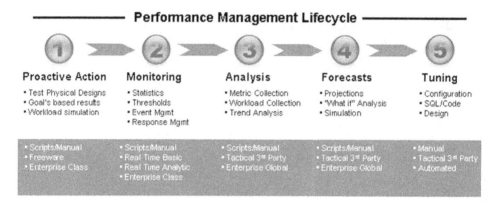

Figure 1.4: *Performance Lifecycle Management.*

Each of these categories will be explained in detail in subsequent chapters, but for now, a quick overview of what makes up each area will be presented.

Proactive Action

The first and most important step in PLM involves in the proactive initiation of action. In upcoming chapters, each of the activities that make up this step will be covered in detail; however, this phase can be boiled down into three key tasks:

- Creating winning physical database designs.

- Stress testing database designs and accompanying system components. According to information compiled by Gartner group, only 10% of IT professionals are actively performance testing their database servers prior to the first day of production.

- Instituting change control to protect proven physical designs and configuration settings.

Success in these three endeavors can lead to great performing SQL Server systems. Conversely, failure to carry these activities out can yield a ticket to disaster.

Monitoring

To be successful at monitoring the SQL Server, the DBA needs to understand the three major performance methodologies:

- Bottleneck Analysis
- Workload Analysis
- Ratio Analysis

Once the DBA has a handle on these methodologies, they can be applied in both ad-hoc and 24 x 7 styles of monitoring. Upcoming chapters in this book will define each of the three performance methodologies. In addition, the processes of applying them in a SWAT-style monitoring way as well as in a continuous around-the-clock fashion will be presented.

Analysis

The DBA can only go so far in the pursuit of looking at data in real time. Only by compiling storage, usage, and performance metrics over time can one detect trends that could, one day, lead to database server outages or serious performance issues.

Unfortunately, according to the Gartner group, only 30% of database professionals actually collect and analyze data in trend analysis fashion. This means that many DBAs are shooting in the dark when it comes to understanding whether things are getting better or worse on their production servers.

An upcoming chapter will explore the importance of properly performing capacity planning, with plenty of information being given on what to collect and when to collect it.

Forecasting

Does the average DBA know how much more storage space will be needed in six months on a particular SQL Server or SAN that serves database servers? Can that DBA easily tell if a certain production server is going to hit its RAM wall next month? These answers can only be gained through the use of intelligent forecasting. Forecasting, of course, is impossible to do without historically gathered data, so this step relies completely on the previous step of Analysis being carried out.

According to Gartner, only 10% of database professionals are actually engaged in the process of forecasting, which means few are really being responsible in their attempts to understand the future needs of their critical database systems.

Tuning

Monitoring and Tuning are likely the two most practiced disciplines in the performance lifecycle. This can be unfortunate for the health of the database, as tuning often relies on understanding stress tests as well as historically gathered performance data. Although there are certainly many items that can be tuned on a database server, the three most frequently visited areas are:

- Configuration.
- SQL Code.
- Physical Design.

In upcoming chapters, tuning will be covered in greater detail. But for now, what about the automatic tuning and diagnostic functions which are supposedly built into SQL Server and other database engines? Aren't these functions going to do away with the need for tuning and possibly even managing a database server?

What about Self-Managing Databases?

What about the whole concept of self-managing databases? Have Microsoft and the other database vendors made the need for Performance Lifecycle Management obsolete by embedding new automatic functionality within the database engine? Hardly.

The recent shift in the major database vendors' marketing messages has been interesting. For years, it used to be that the two primary themes of any new database release centered on performance and scalability. This made sense because each database vendor understood that nearly every corporation's datastores were expanding at exponential levels, hence the touch point for scalability. Additionally, the need for speed with respect to application response times continued to be severe in nearly every environment, thus the performance concentration.

While performance and scalability are still trumpeted by the database giants, they are now overshadowed by a focus on manageability. This can be seen in the releases of IBM DB2 UDB version 8 and Oracle database 10g, both of which tout the self-managing features of the database. Microsoft SQL Server has ridden this same concept in a quieter fashion especially since version 7.0, and it continues in SQL Server 2005.

It is not surprising that such messaging is being put forth right now. Much of this recent push can be traced back to economics. The turbulent economy has, during the early 2000's, caused many IT managers to shift focus from "bigger and better" to cost control. Given the changed corporate mindset, the database vendors find themselves in a position of needing to convince IT management that their databases are not complex or expensive to purchase and manage.

This need has translated into a number of enhancements to the database engine which eases the burden on the DBA in the areas of setup, configuration, administration, and backup/recovery.

However, new smoke signals are being sent up about how databases are soon to be plug-and-play with little to no management being necessary at all like some network cards for a PC. Is such a thing true? In the coming age of self-managing databases, is the SQL Server DBA likely to become obsolete? And what does self-managing really mean anyway?

The following section will address these questions and attempt to clear up the confusion that is leading to many misunderstandings about the self-management capabilities of today's databases.

What Self-Managing Does Mean

When the DBMS vendors say their database is self-managing, to what, exactly, are they referring? From a global perspective, there appear to be several major and minor focuses in the design of self-managing databases, with many of the capabilities centered on performance management and general administration.

The DBMS vendors know that today's DBA spends a large amount of time troubleshooting the performance of their database, so a lot of the self-management direction is in the area of automatic problem diagnosis, communication of diagnostic findings, and generated recommendations on how to fix identified problems.

For example, with the release of DB2 UDB version 8, IBM began offering new built-in features that help locate database inefficiencies and notify the DBA of any performance abnormalities.

At the September 2003 OracleWorld, Oracle first showcased the new Oracle10g self-management features, many of which deal with performance-related issues. The 10g database diagnostic monitor constantly polls a target database, collects critical performance and SQL execution metrics, and then produces formatted reports on any identified performance inefficiencies. 10g has also extended its event handling capabilities to include proactive messages that warn a DBA of impending trouble.

Microsoft SQL Server has had decent event handling embedded with its database for a while, although it lacks the automatic performance diagnostic abilities of IBM and Oracle. Microsoft has come out with a Best Practices Analyzer utility, but it requires manual DBA intervention and is not actually part of the database engine itself.

Other self-managing enhancements are directed at simplifying database installation, configuration, and storage management. These are other areas that can also eat away at a DBA's time. For example, Oracle10g has condensed many of its memory configuration parameters into one that manages the auto-distribution of memory to the areas that need it the most. SQL Server has had this feature for quite some time!

Oracle also now has the ability to automatically stripe, balance, and re-balance a target database over a set of server hard disks to lessen the possibility of I/O hotspots. This is something SQL Server cannot do.

The final list of self-managing enhancements includes things like automatic object statistical updates, which is new in 10g but has been present in SQL Server since version 7.0, and enhanced recovery features that allow the DBA to do partial or near-complete database recoveries without retrieving backup files from other locations.

What Self-Managing Does *Not* Mean

While the enhancements mentioned above are likely to get applause from DBAs and IT managers alike, the majority of critical database tasks and decisions still, and will probably always, require a trained DBA's hand. Those thinking that the new self-management features will do away with the requirement for good DBAs are quite wrong. No matter how self-managing a database is, it will never be able to:

Design Itself: An experienced administrator or data architect is still needed to intelligently create the logical and physical design of a database for real world use. This applies even with auto-storage management.

Build Itself: An administrator will always be needed to smartly implement a physical database design and configure server resource constraints so it can stand up against today's demanding applications.

Secure Itself: Security management is still a process that must be carefully carried out under a trained administrator's eye.

Develop Itself: Many DBAs are called upon to help write or troubleshoot database procedural logic that is produced by a development/application staff.

Change Itself: A database cannot perform true automatic change control in terms of: smartly adding/dropping table columns; reworking security; changing index strategies, although the engines are getting better at this; or altering stored procedural code.

Test Itself: The concept of proper performance testing is not only foreign to the self-management aspects of database engines, but sadly to many DBAs as well.

Recover Itself: Yes, the automated functions of backup and recovery are much better than they were in the past. However, an administrator is still needed to properly set up, monitor, and oversee critical backup and recovery procedures.

No matter how far down the manageability path a database evolves, the disciplines mentioned above make it impossible for a serious production database to ever truly manage itself in the literal sense. Even in the areas of self-managed performance and storage, the latest releases of the database engines are not 100% complete.

The Real Benefits of Self-Managing Databases

This is not to say that the new self-managing features being introduced are not beneficial. On the contrary, they are needed - and indeed must occur, for a variety of reasons.

First, self-managing features are necessary because today's DBA is simply overworked. Embarcadero Technologies conducted many polls of their 70,000+ users and have found that over half of all DBAs manage a least 20 databases, with about a quarter handling 50 or more databases. Unless things change in terms of how corporations use data, these numbers are expected to grow.

One of their large customers has, over the past year, experienced a 60% database growth on their mainframe, but a near 170% growth on their distributed database platforms. Even with all this growth, they have thus far been prevented from hiring any new DBA talent. All of this makes for many long days for the existing DBA staff.

This is where self-managing enhancements can help. By assisting with performance and storage-related duties, some of the administration burden can be taken off the DBA's back. Hopefully the end result will be the DBA having more time to competently manage an increasing database farm, with less time needed to accomplish some previously time-consuming tasks.

Another benefit is that self-managing features may help DBAs adopt other new DBMS enhancements more quickly. Often, a DBA will migrate to a newer version of a database engine but fail to take advantage of the many new features offered in the product. Such situations needlessly drain a busy DBA's time. Hopefully, self-managing databases will ease the burden of database administration so DBAs can investigate and implement features that will save them even more time and trouble in the future.

All of this, of course, comes with the caveat that the self-managing enhancements actually work as advertised. If the database does not automatically direct memory to where it is needed the most or does not correctly balance storage, the DBA will quickly switch off these auto-pilot mechanisms and assume manual control again.

So are self-managing databases welcome? Absolutely. In fact, they are necessary if today's DBA is to make it past keeping their head just above water.

Will Self-Managing Databases Make the DBA Obsolete?

The disciplines and tasks that will always require a seasoned DBA's hand have already been covered, so this question has already been answered in the negative. However, to go further, even in the areas of self-managed performance and storage, there are indicators that DBA intervention is necessary as well.

If the DBA wants to know which way the wind is blowing in terms of databases becoming plug-and-play, even in the areas of performance management, these simple questions can be asked:

- **Is the vendor documentation set shrinking or growing?** Simplification and auto-management would seem to cause the database doc sets to shrink, yet that does not appear to be happening.

- **Are the consulting and DBMS service units getting business?** Ease-of-use brings about a decline in the need for expert help, yet the popular consulting groups and the database vendor's own consulting practices seem to have no trouble obtaining new clients.

- **Have database chat boards gone silent?** The DBA's cries for help will only appear on database chat/help boards if there are still complex and puzzling issues that have to be addressed, and right now, there is plenty of conversation occurring on the popular online forums. For example, Microsoft SQL Server has the reputation of being one of the easier platforms to manage in terms of troubleshooting performance; however, one visit to SQL Server Magazine's online forum will reveal over 2,500 posts dealing with performance topics. This is more than any other area of the site with the single exception being general administration. This begs the question: if SQL Server can self-manage performance so well, why would there be 2,500+ posts on the topic?

Even in the areas of self-managed performance, there is strong evidence that the DBA presence is still very much required. Add to that the fact that DBAs will still be necessary for all the other areas like physical design, change control, performance testing, and others, and one quickly realizes that the need for DBAs is stronger than ever.

In fact, an article in Business 2.0 magazine, "A Job Boom is Coming", September 2003, lists the DBA profession as one of the fastest growing and necessary jobs from now until 2010, with an anticipated growth rate of nearly 70%.

Clearly, DBAs are not obsolete now, nor will they be in the foreseeable future. The self-managing features of the major database vendors are necessary to keep pace with the continuous explosion of corporate data, but the self-management concept does not remove the need for experienced administrators and the valuable benefits they will always provide.

Conclusion

The successful high performance SQL Server DBA will focus more attention on each area of the data lifecycle, especially as the role and responsibilities of the DBA expand into areas where administrators have not traditionally been as actively involved.

In terms of successfully ensuring the optimal performance of the SQL Servers under their care, DBAs must diligently adhere to Performance Lifecycle Management (PLM) and work hard in the areas of:

- Proactive Action.

- Monitoring.

- Analysis.

- Forecasting.

- Tuning.

Each stage is critical and cannot be discarded if continual success in the area of performance management is desired.

The next chapter will present methods and thoughts on how to accurately measure the performance of a SQL Server, so the DBA will know exactly what to be looking for when it comes to measuring the performance of a system.

Accurately Assessing Database Performance

Introduction

Probably every SQL Server professional would like to be thought of as a performance-tuning expert. Slow systems are the bane of existence for any critical business, and DBAs and developers alike constantly strive to improve their diagnostic skills. And, why shouldn't they? The IT consultants who make the big money are the ones who can take a lethargic system and quickly turn it into one that runs as fast as lightning.

While there is certainly a lot of theory and information flying back and forth in books, magazines, and on database bulletin boards, the fact is the majority of database administrators are confused over how they should really monitor a database to ensure peak efficiency.

To make matters worse, the continual march towards complexity of the major DBMS vendors, such as the SQL Server, means that today's database professional must constantly stay abreast of new performance issues. Add to the mix that most DBAs must work cross-platform and that the number of databases they manage is skyrocketing, one quickly finds that the stage is set with the makings of a real mess.

Due to today's heavy reliance on database-driven systems, a database professional cannot waste time guessing at what might be causing a critical database to sputter and cough along like a 1912 Model T Ford. Instead, they need to understand the performance priorities of a

---

database, and be able to quickly and proactively identify problems before they reach a critical point.

One of the best ways to understand such a concept is by modeling database performance. While modeling a database design might be a familiar concept, the idea of creating a model of database performance might seem odd at first. Can something like this actually be done?

Modeling Peak Efficiency

Models represent the big picture of something on the surface. They also provide methods to drill down into the nitty-gritty of a subject. Data models, for example, are a way to succinctly communicate the aspects and aspect-relationships of a database in a way that even non-technical folks can usually understand.

A performance model is designed to do the same. Its purpose is to communicate the total performance situation, using a direct method, in a way that both the experienced and novice database staff member can understand. A model of this nature should, for example, be able to quickly convey a total performance message, so that the DBA knows exactly where they stand and what their tuning priorities must be. Accomplishing this requires zeroing in on the major aspects of database performance and working downward from there.

Stating the obvious, it can be said that the goal of every database professional is to achieve peak efficiency in their database. So just what is peak efficiency? One way to define it is with the simple formula:

```
PEAK EFFICIENCY = AVAILABILITY + SPEED
```

Availability and speed combine to make or break any database system. This is true regardless of the underlying architecture of the database engine. DBAs need their databases to be up and their resources available in order to meet incoming requests. They also need the DBMS configured so that it can quickly handle all imposed system loads. While

---

this may look simple on the surface, it is much more complicated under that surface.

The performance model, regardless of whether it is an SQL Server or other DBMS platform, begins with the two critical elements of availability and speed. If a method can be found to quickly diagnose their success or failure, the DBA will be on the way to working more efficiently.

Modeling Availability

Many professionals have the erroneous assumption that because a database server is up, it is available. Nothing could be further from the truth. There are many factors that need to be considered when modeling the availability portion of the performance model. Although other factors may play a part, the computation of database availability can be summed up in the equation:

```
TOTAL AVAILABILITY = DATABASE SERVER ACCESSIBILITY +
  RESOURCE AVAILABILITY
```

Each availability component is comprised of several sub-modules that must be measured. For database server accessibility, there are two primary components, database server readiness and connectivity.

Database Server Accessibility

The two primary components that make up database server accessibility are:

- **Database Server Readiness**: This component is what everyone thinks of when the question is asked, "Is the SQL Server up"? This equates to the SQL Server service being successfully started, background processes plus memory structures, and having all file structures accounted for and open.

- **Connectivity:** It is amazing how often people forget about the network side of the database server. This does not mean LANs or

TCP, but the required components that allow client connections into a database. This boils down to being able to log into the SQL Server via the embraced DBLIB network utilities and network protocol (named pipes, TCP, etc).

Once accessibility to the database server is established, the next area to peer into is resource availability.

Resource Availability

Like database server accessibility, resource availability is made up of two factors. These factors are space resource availability and object resource availability.

Space Resource Availability

If a database does not have enough space to respond to data additions or modifications, it is basically not available except for, perhaps, read operations. Even these may be impacted if a disk sort is necessary to complete a *select* request.

In addition to space concerns inside the database, space outside the database must also be taken into account, especially in this age where database files automatically grow to accommodate heavier than expected data loads. Make no mistake; space availability contributes much to the overall availability of any database.

Object Resource Availability

In almost every database system, the DBA will find a hub table that passes critical data in and out. Such systems are not difficult to bring to a standstill. All it takes is a table being reorganized, an index becoming corrupt, or other such acts, and true database availability goes out the window. Many other factors can affect resource availability as well.

DBAs who have spent considerable time in their profession will, no doubt, have occasionally encountered a blocking lock tree that is a mile long usually consisting of one user blocking out everyone else, users waiting on memory structures to open up, or other contention events that affect overall efficiency. Total availability is heavily impacted by how available the critical resources used by the database are kept. It often affects the speed of the database as well.

Regardless of the database engine being used, the performance model needed will consist of an availability sub-model that is comprised of the aforementioned elements. For most critical businesses, availability is the first priority. Only after availability is confirmed can speed become the focus.

Modeling Speed

As mentioned, all DBAs desire a fast and well-performing database. But, exactly how does the DBA gauge database speed? Is a 99% buffer cache hit ratio the litmus test, or is it more complicated than that? Modeling the components of the speed sub-model is basically straightforward, but there are some difficult to measure items that must be taken into account. To measure the success of the speed sub-model, the following equation will be used:

```
DATABASE SPEED = ACCESS EFFICIENCY + CODE EFFICIENCY +
  DESIGN SUCCESS
```

If the request completion rate and code efficiency ranking are at peak levels and the database design is correct for the situation, the database will likely be a top performer. As with the total availability model, the two main speed model components consist of several subcomponents.

Access Efficiency

The two components that define access efficiency are data/code positioning and access path effectiveness.

Data/Code Positioning

Data, code, and object definitions that reside in memory have a much higher return rate than objects that must first be retrieved from disk and placed into memory. The latest numbers on this topic suggest that data can be accessed from RAM around 1,400 times faster than on physical disk.

While database engines differ in the layout of the memory structures used to hold data and other necessary items, they all contain areas that function to speed the delivery of data and to lookup information. The percentage of times the database can serve information from memory instead of disk will contribute mightily toward overall database speed. Things such as data being available in the SQL Server cache and stored procedure definitions being nestled into memory all play a part.

Of course, hardware design counts, too. Fast drives and load segmentation both play a part. Contention at this level; however, normally falls under resource availability.

Access Path Effectiveness

The second determinant of access efficiency is the route through which the information must travel to be accessed. Index lookups versus table scans must be taken into account to determine how well code has been written or how well the DBMS optimizer chooses the best path. Design considerations also come into play.

Small table scans should be overlooked, as it is often more efficient for a database to cache and scan a small table than to use any available indexing mechanisms. Another important factor that contributes to access path effectiveness is the consistent application of object demographics to the data dictionary.

Most DBAs have witnessed an access path, which worked well for objects with a certain volume of data, begin to fail when the demographics of those objects changed and the database's optimizer was not informed of the change.

The final huge factor is I/O consumption, which is comprised of logical and physical consumption. While physical I/O may take longer to accomplish a database request, a heavy load of logical I/O is not conducive to quick response time either. Mitigating both should be a goal of the performance model. Even if the database is servicing requests well in memory, it might not matter if the code is not accessing the data properly or utilizing the right techniques to get only the data that is necessary.

This is the point at which some DBAs who rely only on singular measures, such as the cache hit ratio, fail to properly measure performance. Yes, a user thread may sport a 98% cache hit ratio, but if that same thread used 500,000 logical reads to produce a result that SQL could have achieved in 5,000 logical reads, wouldn't overall speed be increased with the use of SQL?

Measuring code efficiency is not simple since individual SQL statements can be difficult to track and trace; however, there are a few components that will indicate positive or negative trends in this territory. The following section provides some details on these components.

Code Efficiency

The three areas to review with respect to code efficiency are system balance, code reuse and code soundness/validation.

System Balance

Many rules of thumb turn out to be untrue, but the one saying, "80% of the problems in a database are caused by 10-20% of the users" is right on the money. Rarely will the DBA encounter a database in which a majority of users and their SQL statements produce extreme negative code-related performance statistics. Instead, a few sessions and their accompanying SQL will be the culprits degrading performance. That being the case, the percentage of code-related statistics (memory and disk I/O) of the current resource hogs versus the system total can be evaluated to see how balanced the code is with respect to performance.

Code Reuse

Except in the most ad-hoc databases, code reuse should be encouraged and enforced. Depending on the DBMS engine, this can be accomplished in a variety of ways, such as:

- Maintaining procedural code through the use of stored procedures and triggers. This is applicable to SQL Server as well as most other platforms.

- Embedding SQL code in applications to ensure all user sessions are running the same code line.

Why is code reuse important? Myriads of untested and untuned SQL statements sent against a database have the potential to cause performance bottlenecks. In addition, the DBMS engine must work extra hard at parsing and security checks. Techniques outlined later in this book will reveal how to accomplish code reuse without working up too much of a sweat.

Code Soundness/Validation

While it is difficult to gauge the validity of a piece of database code in a computational method, there are telltale signs. Long execution times associated with seemingly simple code can raise eyebrows, as can skyrocketing logical or physical I/O for code runs. In addition, the invalidation of code objects can cause terrible malfunctions in a system. Invalid code objects simply have no place in a production system. Period.

Design Success

Many DBAs believe that code inefficiency is the number one cause of system problems. As previously mentioned, many rules of thumb turn out to be untrue, and this is one of them.

The number one cause of performance-related problems, as well as system outages, is simply bad design. Tragically, this is not only the number one cause of speed and availability headaches, but it is also the most difficult to model in terms of declaring a database design good or bad overall.

For example, how can the DBA easily tell if denormalizing a set of tables into one object will accelerate performance? In the world of RAID and fast I/O devices, how can it be known whether separating tables and indexes onto different physical drives will enhance speed, or if another index is needed on a large dimension-styled table?

Unfortunately, design success cannot be measured as easily or evaluated as quickly as the other components in the performance model. However, an upcoming chapter in this book will explain how to identify physical design weaknesses that ultimately lead to reduced system performance.

Model Dependencies

The goal of the performance model, as well as any other model, is to communicate the total picture in an easily assimilated form. Therefore, the goal of the performance model is to provide the database professional with a global view of peak efficiency, either for a single database or a large number of installations. How will this be accomplished? Figure 2.1 presents a bird's eye view of how the DBA can globally gauge the peak efficiency of any database.

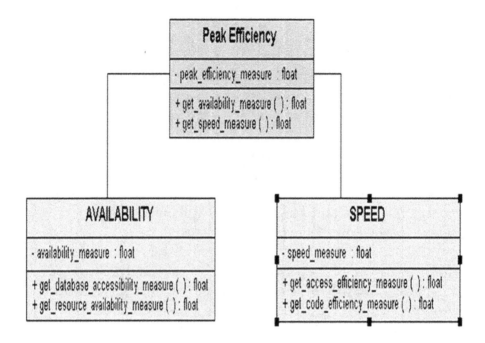

Figure 2.1: *Abbreviated global performance model representing the components of peak efficiency.*

To indicate peak efficiency, the model in Figure 2.1 uses a single peak efficiency measure to communicate the overall health of the database system. While this is certainly functional, the two measures derived from the availability and speed classes can also be used.

Why would this be a desirable approach? The reason is that speed becomes irrelevant if total availability is not close to maximum levels. Using a single indicator to convey peak efficiency might be more efficient; however, if the DBA is called upon to evaluate many systems at once, using the two measures independent of one another is possible as well. Of course, speed will not be a factor if the database is not accessible.

Following in this vein, one should note that dependencies or relationships will exist in the performance model. As with any model, rarely are there objects that operate independently.

If an entity has no relationship with other entities in the data model being constructed, why would it be included in the model? Those working in the data modeling discipline generally frown upon entities left dangling in a model. Any good performance model has relationships or dependencies that are of critical importance. Performance modeling succeeds where traditional performance monitoring fails because it takes into account the dependencies between the many performance classes and measures. Only when a DBA observes both the measurements and the effect each has on the other will the true performance picture emerge.

It is a fact that peak efficiency cannot be measured simply by weighing availability and speed independent of one another. It has already been stated that speed is of no concern in a down database server. Yet, if a database is accessible and resources are open to incoming requests, speed quickly becomes the primary focus of attention. Figure 2.2 displays the dependency links in the performance model.

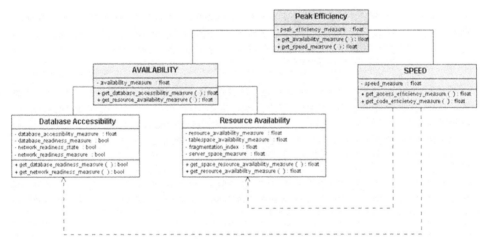

Figure 2.2: *Availability sub-model showing dependency links of speed to availability.*

Speed depends on the overall availability. However, the various dependencies will differ in their strength ratings, which is why the dependency links are drawn from the speed class to the availability sub-classes.

For example, if either the database server or network is not in a ready state, no real work in a database can be performed. Speed's contribution to overall peak efficiency is totally negated. If, on the other hand, the database server is accessible, but certain resources are unavailable, or nearly unavailable, speed may be impacted. However, its contribution is not totally removed from the peak efficiency equation.

Issues like a full database transaction log can produce nearly the same effect as a down database. But, common resource issues such as a database file nearing the end of its free space amount will not impact the speed class in the model nearly as much as database server accessibility.

Still, resource availability has the ability to become a showstopper in any database. It is a good bet that if the database is configured well and has the right design in place, but still has bottlenecks and slowdowns in the system, the probable root cause will be waits and other resource blocks. Given poor resource availability, speed can again become a non-issue.

The Impact of Availability

How does availability impact the performance model? The best way to grasp this concept is to delve into several different availability-related situations and examine their impact on the performance model.

Of course, the first situation to consider is what happens when the database server suddenly goes down. The impact of this situation is fairly easy to assess. When the availability suddenly drops to zero, the peak efficiency of the database would be at zero as well.

While database server accessibility components have the potential to cause a sudden, catastrophic drop in the peak efficiency model, other components can crash a system just as easily, but the end of the story will not be quite as abrupt. One case to consider could involve lock contention, one of the building blocks of resource availability.

What happens to the model when lock contention rears its ugly head? The answer is dependent on a couple of factors:

- The ratio of blocked users (database work) to overall connected sessions.

- The duration of the bottleneck.

In the case of a database with 300 connected sessions and a current peak efficiency level of ninety-eight percent, resource availability comes under fire when a single session grabs a resource and retains it for a short duration. Ten or so other sessions queue up quickly behind the blocking session and wait on the resource. The resource is released by the original blocking session in short order, which then allows the other ten user threads to complete their work, and things return to normal. This brief encounter with lock contention would likely cause barely a hiccup in overall peak efficiency.

But, lock contention cases can be more severe. In the case of a database that is running at ninety-eight percent peak efficiency but only has twenty user sessions performing work, one of the sessions locks a hub table. Before the resource is released, the session owner is suddenly called into a long meeting.

One by one, the remaining active sessions queue up behind the blocking session until all are waiting. With both the blocked user/total connection ratio and lock duration measures working against the database, peak efficiency begins an overall downhill slide until it reaches zero or near-zero.

Where does speed fit into this picture? Again, speed is totally negated by its dependency on the two main components that make up availability.

Does it matter how high memory access measures are or that the access paths the optimizer is using to retrieve data couldn't be better?

Not in this case. Peak efficiency is, in effect, brought to a standstill by a single, escalating case of lock contention. The same statement could also be made of a transactional-heavy database suffering from a full transaction log.

The point of this exercise has been threefold. First, it has served to show that intelligent factors must be put into the performance model so each component and measure can accurately reflect the impact of circumstances that influence overall peak efficiency. In other words, the relationships/dependencies between measures play a huge role in communication performance.

Second, it has underscored the critical nature of availability, and why it should always be the DBA's number one priority.

But lastly and most importantly, it has demonstrated the extremely important benefit of a performance model, which is to represent performance as the end user is experiencing it.

When a legitimate problem call comes in, many times the DBA will pull up a script or monitor and look at individual statistics that, by themselves, mean little or nothing. "Everything looks OK to me," the DBA says. When pressed by the anxious user, however, the DBA might dig a little deeper and finally discover the bottleneck. In an ideal world, the DBA would have the ability to instantly see the situation as the end user sees it.

The Impact of Speed

One might look at this performance model and think, "Well, speed doesn't seem to matter much at all in this model." This simply is not true. If there is a database server with accessibility nearly always ensured and with resource availability at peak levels around the clock, does that mean peak efficiency is not at risk? No, of course not. Speed becomes the all-important component of the performance model when and only when availability is under control. After availability is assured, speed becomes king.

The phone call most DBAs hate is the one that starts off with the complaint "Gee, the database sure seems to be running slow!" Of course, the network, application, and various other stress points could not be the problem. It always has to be the database, right? For the moment, remove all other mitigating factors and consider a situation where there actually is something going on at the database level.

What does slow mean? Slow could mean results from a SELECT statement are not coming back in reasonable amount of time, the heavy-duty procedure that is doing some serious number crunching is not completing within historical timeframes, or a process just seems to hang. The first two symptoms generally fall into the area of speed, while the last problem is typically one of resource availability.

Speed's impact on the overall peak efficiency model will seldom reduce the overall measure to zero or near zero, but low speed ratings in the performance model can certainly make life miserable for users. How can the overall impact of speed be measured? First, availability has no such dependencies tied to speed.

It is important to understand that speed, as it is defined in the performance model, does not come into play with issues like how fast an incident of lock contention is resolved or the quickness at which a database's free space is restored. Speed is comprised of how quickly and effectively data is accessed, the efficiency of a database's code line, and the success of the physical database design.

As with availability, the various components and building blocks of speed cannot be weighted in some static nature. Some will count more than others, depending on the particular personality of the database and the total work being done at the moment. For example, nearly every

SQL Server professional has watched database performance suffer at the hands of a user who has executed a massive procedure or runaway query.

Such a situation could signal problems in either the access or code efficiency components of the performance model. More than likely, it is a code imbalance in the system, which would fall under the code efficiency portion of the model. While the problem procedure or query would temporarily depress measures like a cache hit ratio or other memory statistics, the root cause of overall speed degradation is a piece of code out of balance with the normal work being conducted on a system.

Conclusion

A thorough understanding of the impact that each type of performance dependency has on the database is necessary when figuring out how to gauge database performance excellence. As is so often the case, however, the devil is in the details when it comes to troubleshooting a complex database. The following points are key to such troubleshooting:

- **Modeling Peak Efficiency**: This is defined with the simple formula:

  `PEAK EFFICIENCY = AVAILABILITY + SPEED.`

- **Modeling Availability**: Although other factors may play a part, the computation of database availability can be summed up in the equation:

  `TOTAL AVAILABILITY = DATABASE SERVER ACCESSIBILITY + RESOURCE AVAILABILITY.`

- **Modeling Speed**: To measure the success of the speed sub-model, the following equation is used:

  `DATABASE SPEED = ACCESS EFFICIENCY + CODE EFFICIENCY + DESIGN SUCCESS.`

- **Model Dependencies**: The goal of the performance model is to provide the database professional with a global view of peak efficiency, either for a single database or a large number of installations.

The remainder of this book is devoted to helping the DBA focus on, and drill down into, the major areas of database availability and speed so that troubled systems can be restored to peak efficiency as quickly as possible. This is accomplished by adhering to each stage of the performance management lifecycle.

Whether it is uncovering physical design issues that are cramping overall performance or pinpointing table scans that are wreaking havoc at the I/O level, methodologies, techniques, and scripts will be presented that can be used to ferret out the root cause of performance slowdowns on any SQL Server system.

The next chapter will focus on the first step of performance lifecycle management, which is the proactive actions stage. Without question, neglecting this step has caused more grief to a DBA than any other. If this step is executed properly, much of the performance battle is over; however, if it is ignored or not taken seriously, a rough road ahead is guaranteed.

Performance Lifecycle Management: Step One

Proactive Actions that Ensure Optimized Performance

The first step in Performance Lifecycle Management (PLM) centers on proactive actions that lay the foundation for a successful SQL Server implementation. There are three key activities in this step with which database administrators need to become exceptionally skilled if they desire to be high performance SQL Server DBAs. The three keys are:

- Physical Database Design

- Proactive Performance Testing

- Change Management

These three disciplines are challenging to carry out, but they are vital to the optimized performance of any SQL Server driven system. The following section begins with information on what is, by far, the single most important contributor to database performance: physical database design.

Laying a Strong Foundation

Perhaps one of the largest benefits of working as a Database Tools Engineer is having the opportunity to witness great examples of "how not to do it." One particular engagement that can be used as an illustration involved a client who was having a terrible problem with query response time from both his custom-built GUI and ad-hoc reporting tools. He stated that the response time required to receive a query result could exceed an hour or more for some reports. Clearly, something had to change.

After reviewing the problem, the first thing that had to be done was the running of a complete set of database diagnostics, as well as server diagnostics, after which the results were analyzed. A number of definite problems were found in both the placement of database files and the discovery of heavy database fragmentation, which no doubt contributed to the overall response time problem.

However, this was not sufficient to cause such poor performance. There had to be something else that was the main culprit for such a pronounced lag in response time. As would logically happen in such a case, one of the typical reports that had been requested was reviewed in detail. The report included a fairly complex query that joined a number of database views. On the surface, nothing appeared out of the ordinary. Yet, it was only upon closer examination of the underlying views that the problem began to surface.

The first view used in the report was simply amazing in scope and complexity. It involved a selection of 43 columns that joined 33 tables and had a join predicate that contained not less than 28 outer joins. This was just one view involved with the report!

The important point in this example is that even if every database tuning guideline for building a system is followed closely, but the physical database design is wrong, the system will fail. The database described above was suffering from a case of extreme normalization. Instead of recognizing and addressing their poor design, the project leaders had hoped to see some quick tuning magic that would set things right.

Unfortunately, their solution would not be that easy. Isn't it ironic that in an attempt to improve performance, many companies turn to highly paid database consultants and spend tens of thousands of dollars on database performance monitors that track thousands of statistics, only to be left shaking their heads at a system that still crawls along? As a SQL Server professional, the one question to always keep in mind when examining a database's performance, "What is the actual physical design?"

The following section addresses the critical importance of database design and demonstrates how some of the problems the database is currently experiencing are the result of an improper physical model.

Why is Physical Design Overlooked?

When troubleshooting performance problems, why is it that the physical database design is so often overlooked? The primary reason is that most DBAs have been taught that bad SQL or insufficient resources (hardware, memory, etc.) are usually the main culprits in poor database performance. It is easier to hunt for bad SQL and throw hardware at a slow-running database than to investigate a database's physical design for the following two reasons:

- A proper physical design is difficult to construct.

- A proper physical design takes time and sometimes lots of it.

Sometimes a DBA is stymied by a purchased application situation in which they are bequeathed a design that they have no control over, or so it seems. However, there are times when physical design tweaks can be made at the indexing level if such customizations do not void any agreements with the purchased application's vendor.

When data modelers begin creating a non-RDBMS specific database design, the model is labeled as a logical design. The modelers work diligently at normalization, in which they ensure the model is relationally accurate. This means that all entities have primary keys; all attributes in an entity depend on the primary key, etc. That design is then often turned over to DBAs for the creation of a physical design, which is a specifically targeted model for a particular RDBMS, such as SQL Server.

Designing a high performance database is complicated work. It takes skill and experience to develop a design that runs efficiently. The unfortunate truth is that experienced database personnel are at a premium these days, so junior or completely novice IT workers are called upon to design and build databases.

The corporate mindset of retaining a staff of experienced logical data modelers was all but thrown out in the early nineties when a then prominent tool company promised everything under the sun but cracked under the strain of real world business models. Since many of the company's tools failed to deliver as promised and the designers of these tools stressed logical design as the necessary forerunner of a good system, logical design was discounted with respect to its importance.

Corporations had endured so many logical design projects that never got off the drawing board that Rapid Application Development (RAD) became the accepted mode of development. The end result was, and still is today, that logical and physical design are not taken nearly as seriously in overall system development as they should.

The second reason quality designs are overlooked when the topic of performance is discussed is that a considerable amount of up-front time is needed to create a good design, and time is not what most companies have these days. The application lifecycle has never been shorter in corporations than it is right now.

Projects that would have taken years to complete merely five years ago are being completed in six months or less. To accomplish such a feat requires one of two things: superior personnel using state-of-the art software tools; or the elimination of necessary tasks from the application construction equation.

Usually, one of the first compromises is the abandonment of the database logical design phase. The reason for this is that project leaders believe that all will be well if the database is designed in parallel with the application code. Instead of taking the time to intelligently lay out the necessary components and objects of a database, the database structure is built in the development phase alongside the code base used to run the application. The end result is poor design.

Instead of concentrating on good physical database design, database professionals look to other methods to enhance performance. As they look the wrong way, they risk overlooking the problem and end up with a database that simply will not perform.

The Number One Performance Myth

Whether it's in the realm of database technology or any other discipline, some maxims are circulated in hushed tones so much that they are taken literally as fact and never questioned, especially when supposed experts mouth the words. Such is the case with the following database performance myth:

"Eighty percent of a database's overall performance is derived from the code that is written against it."

This is a complete untruth, or at the very least, an overestimation of the impact that properly written SQL code has against a running physical database. Good coding practices definitely count, often heavily, toward the success of any database application; however, to state affirmatively that they make a contribution of over two-thirds is a stretch.

The reason this cannot pass the reality test is that it is stated independently of what good or bad code can do in the face of poor physical design. The performance problem example presented earlier in this chapter is a shining example of how wrong this adage is.

The physical design constrains all code, good or bad, and has the capability to turn even the best written SQL into virtual molasses. After all, how can an SQL developer obtain unique key index access unless the physical index has been created and is in place? How can a database coder scan only the parts of a table that they need unless that table has been partitioned (SQL Server 2005 and above) to accommodate such a request? Only when a solid physical design is put in place that truly fits the application can SQL code really take off and make for impressive response times. But, good design comes first.

The Link between Performance Monitoring and Physical Design

Every database professional wants to be thought of as an expert in database tuning. The consultants that make the most money in this field are the ones who can miraculously transform a sluggish, wheezing database into one that runs fast and efficiently. The books that fly off the shelf in the technical bookstores are the ones that promise hidden tips on accelerating the performance of database systems.

 A good DBA covets complicated SQL scripts that dig into the heart of a database's internals and regurgitate mountains of difficult-to-interpret statistics. But, do those database DBAs really know what to do with all the information produced through performance monitors and SQL scripts? How does a DBA effectively monitor a database for performance and make a difference in the response time and the user's experience?

The key to understanding the discipline of performance monitoring is this:

When monitoring a database for performance, the DBA is really validating the physical design implementation.

If the performance monitor chosen is blasting the DBA with flashing lights, alarm bells, and pager alerts, it is probably because the physical design is failing. If all is quiet on the scene with the performance monitor, the physical design is likely a current success. It really is almost that simple.

To be sure, there are performance situations that are not impacted by the physical design directly. Lock contention, for example, is mostly an application or coding issue. On a grand scale, the performance monitoring output speaks volumes on the talents of the database designer.

Are there any I/O contention problems in the database? If so, it is likely that the tables and indexes were not physically segmented across different filegroups properly in the physical design.

Are there too many large table scans in the database? Chances are the proper indexing or partitioning strategy was not closely adhered to.

Are either the storage structures or objects causing undo out-of-space headaches? It is a good bet that the database was not sized properly in the initial physical design.

It is in poor judgment to dismiss the idea that altering and improving a database's physical design will yield the largest possible performance benefit.

In part, the reason for this is that modifying the design of a physical database, especially one that is currently in production, is no easy task and often requires substantial amounts of off-hours work by the DBA. Instead, many take the quick fix approach to performance problems. In most cases, this means they simply throw more hardware at the situation. There are three hardware fixes readily available to carry out this task:

- The server box itself can be upgraded.

- More processors can be introduced to the mix.

- Additional RAM can be added.

In the short term, things might appear to get better, and if the database is relatively static in nature, things may remain that way. If the database

---

is dynamic and the data/user load continues to grow, the problem will likely return.

In this instance, the issue is at the foundation level. If the foundation is flawed, the structure needs to be put in order at that level before anything else is done. Unfortunately, performance monitoring and problem resolution today is often not handled that way. It is similar to when a homeowner discovers that his house has a cracked foundation, adds a new coat of paint to cover up the cracks, and then declares that all is well. Even worse, the homeowner attempts to add on to the home in hopes of improving the value or appeal. But who will buy the house with a cracked foundation?

The same premise holds true for adding more hardware onto a poorly designed database. More RAM, etc., can be thrown at a badly performing database, and for a while, those performance cracks are covered up. But over time, as more data and users are added, those foundational cracks will reappear and must be dealt with yet again. Regardless of the effort involved, it is much better to attack the foundation problem first in order to correct the problems permanently.

As an example, a DBA who still practices ratio-based analysis may use the performance monitor to find that the cache hit ratio is far below acceptable levels, typically 80% or less. The DBA may erroneously conclude from the situation that more RAM is needed or that the buffer cache should be enlarged to improve performance.

Instead, what if the problem stems from the fact that too many large table scans are occurring? Most RDBMSs will quickly recycle the data obtained from large table scan operations to keep stale data out of the cache which can be confirmed via SQL Server's Page Life Expectancy performance counter. The issue could be a coding problem in which developers are not using the constructs in the SQL predicates.

More likely, the database may not have the correct indexes in place to assist the code in avoiding the many large table scans. If this physical design flaw can be correctly identified, no extra RAM may be needed.

Is there a link between availability and design? According to Oracle Corporation's own studies of client downtime, the largest percentage, are design-related issues as shown in Figure 3.1. If database design has not been an important issue until now, this should be considered a wake-up call.

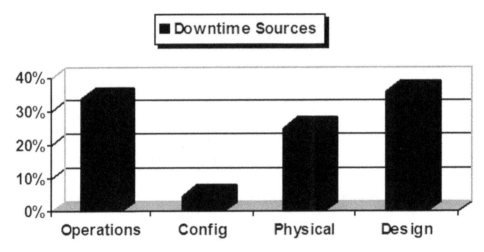

Figure 3.1: *Downtime statistics provided by Oracle Corporation.*

Making the Biggest Performance Impact

Proper physical design should be the number one performance goal for the DBA. It is time to get serious about how to manage the Physical Design Lifecycle.

So, how do DBAs get started in making a noticeable difference in the physical designs of databases currently under their care and those they are destined to encounter and/or build in the future?

The first step is a mental one and involves making the commitment to create excellent physical design in all database applications. In reality, all project management personnel need to make this same commitment, as the effort required to guarantee a solid physical design foundation will take more up-front resources. Make no mistake; to say that this would time well spent is an understatement.

The next step involves education of the database designer. Of course, the best way to become a design guru is to put time in the trenches and work with every style of database available: heavy OLTP, data warehousing, and cross-platform data mart designs. By doing this, the DBA will learn very quickly which designs stand and which physical foundations crack when up against heavy-duty web-based and mega-user systems. Of course, there are also a variety of good educational classes and books on the subject of physical design to aid in the learning process.

 Creating robust, efficient physical designs can be difficult and intricate work. Therefore, the DBA will need to be armed with serious power tools that have the capability to slice through the difficulties involved in building and retrofitting complex physical database designs. Long gone are the days when a DBA or modeler could handle most of their work with an SQL query interface and a drawing tool. Today, relational databases are just too robust and contain too many complexities for such primitive aids.

At a minimum, DBAs will need two items flanking their database arsenal: a serious data modeling tool and a robust performance monitoring product. It has already been established that performance monitoring is really the validation of a database's physical design. When foundational cracks are identified with the monitor, a high-quality design tool to aid in rectifying the situation will be needed.

For those physical DBAs who do not like to use data modeling tools, two other software products will be needed: a feature-rich database administration tool and a change control product. The database administration tool will be used to create new objects for a database as well as modify properties of existing objects. This tool is normally used in an ad-hoc manner and is great for graphically redesigning a database in real-time mode.

The change control product is a different animal. If the DBA will not use a data modeling tool to capture and version control the designs of databases, that person will need another method for protecting designs that are in place and working. Having such snapshot backups of the database's schemas will prove invaluable when disaster strikes. More information will be shared on this in an upcoming section.

Spotting Physical Design Flaws

Once the database design tool arsenal is in place and the system goes into production, the work of building correct physical designs from scratch and managing the physical design lifecycle can begin. How does one quickly spot physical design flaws in an up-and-running database?

While it definitely takes a trained eye to uncover the root cause of performance problems, Table 3.1 will help the DBA get started. It lists just a few of the most common database performance problems and the possible physical design gremlins that could be the culprit in a SQL Server database.

PERFORMANCE CATEGORY	PERFORMANCE PROBLEM	POSSIBLE DESIGN CAUSE
Memory	Poor Cache Hit Ratio	Too many large table scans; invalid indexing scheme. Not enough RAM devoted to buffer cache memory area. Not pinning small lookup tables in memory.
	Bad Memory Sort Ratio	Not presorting data when possible.
	Low Free Cache Percent	Insufficient RAM installed on server.
	Poor Page Life Expectancy Counter Value	Insufficient RAM installed on server. Invalid index strategy.
	Total Server Memory nearing or at Target Server Memory Counter	Insufficient RAM installed on server.
I/O	Identified Disk Contention	Not separating tables and accompanying indexes into different filegroups on different physical drives.
	Slow Access to System Information	Not placing *master* database on little accessed physical drive.
	Slow Disk Sorts	Placing *tempdb* database on RAID5 drive or heavily accessed physical volume.
	Abnormally High Physical I/O	Too many large table scans – invalid indexing scheme. Not enough RAM devoted to buffer cache memory area. Not keeping small lookup tables pinned in the cache.
	High Log Writer Wait Times	Putting log files on RAID5 or heavily accessed physical volumes.

PERFORMANCE CATEGORY	PERFORMANCE PROBLEM	POSSIBLE DESIGN CAUSE
Space	Out of Space Conditions (storage structures)	Poorly forecasted data volumes in physical design. Not enabling auto-grow for database and log files. Database or log files with too-small setting for maximum file size.
	Database/Object Fragmentation	Bad column choices of clustered key indexes.
	Page Splitting	Poor clustered index choice.
SQL	Large JOIN Queries	Over normalized database design.
Object Activity	Forwarded Row Tables	Invalid settings for CHAR or VARCHAR column sizes.
	Many Large Table Scans	Incorrect indexing scheme.
	Object Fragmentation	Bad column choices of clustered key indexes.
	Page Splitting	Poor clustered index choice.

Table 3.1: *Performance Problems and Possible Physical Design Causes.*

Using a quality performance monitor, performance headaches in the database can quickly be discovered; and then, using either an intelligent data-modeling tool or the combination of a database administration/change control product, the situation can be properly remedied.

Fixing foundational flaws in a database is never easy, but perhaps one day the DBA community will be treated to software that gets things right before the situation turns ugly.

Physical Design Conclusion

So, what was done to fix the slow-running database described at the beginning of this section? First, the over-normalization of the database was pointed out to the database modelers and DBAs. Unfortunately, they were not agreeable to working on the design to make things run better. Instead, a small data-mart was created from the transactional database that the end users could work against to build the reports they needed.

A small Extract-Transform-Load (ETL) routine was also written and fronted with an easy to use GUI that the users could run whenever they desired to refresh the data-mart's contents. Where their reports had taken over an hour to run before, the entire ETL process and report process now crossed the finish line in under seven minutes. If the ETL routine did not need to be run, the actual report creation could be accomplished in about two minutes. A better design, suited to the end users needs, was just the ticket to make things right.

The main points of this section include:

- Never compromise a project by neglecting the database's physical design phase.

- Understand that much of a database's performance comes from its physical design foundation.

- When troubleshooting system performance, keep an eye on indicators that signal a problem with the overall database physical design.

How to Build an 'Unbreakable' Database

If it's true that what can go wrong eventually will, then database professionals have to think about what can potentially go wrong with a database so they can take proactive steps to avoid potential problems. It's important to understand that there are two distinct types of overall database problems for which to be on the lookout: showstoppers and performance vampires.

Showstoppers are just what their name implies. When they occur, everything grinds to a halt. They cause the classic database server freeze in which no one can perform any work. Suddenly the calls start to flood in with complaints of application hangs. The most common showstoppers include:

- **Space Outages**: This occurs when the database runs out of available free space in either the database storage structures or at the operating system level. An example would be a Microsoft SQL Server transaction log reaching 100% of capacity or failing to automatically grow due to an insufficient amount of available space on the physical disk.

- **Reaching Resource Limits**: This is what happens when no more locks are available on a SQL Server transaction processing (OLTP) system? Essentially, no one else can do any work and things cease functioning.

- **Lock Contention** – A single escalating case of lock contention has the potential to bottleneck any database in the same manner an accident can cause gridlock on a major interstate. There is probably no more frequent showstopper in a database than a runaway case of lock contention.

Performance vampires differ from showstoppers in that they gradually drain a database of its performance over time as opposed to instantly stopping a database in its tracks. They can also give the appearance of 'good enough' performance when, in reality, better throughput can be achieved by changing various areas of a database's design or configuration.

These gremlins are harder to plan for and proactively nip in the bud because they often do not rear their heads unless certain factors come into play, a consistent load is placed on the database, or a database slowly begins to break down and show signs of 'age'. The most common performance vampires include:

- **I/O and File Contention** – When database files are initially placed on a server, they may have been balanced well from an I/O standpoint, but over time as new files are added or increased load is placed on the original physical design, contention can begin to cause unacceptable response times.

- **CPU and Memory Exhaustion** – Although most database professionals would not admit it, they often play a guessing game when it comes to specifying the CPU and memory assignments for a new database. More is sometimes *not* better, and database planners that find this out the hard way can get quite frustrated. However, if the number/capacity of CPUs and the amount of memory assigned to a database are not sufficient, it may exhibit sluggishness from day one of production.

- **Database Object Fragmentation** – When first created; database tables and indexes are usually in terrific shape. However, over time as INSERT, UPDATE and DELETE activity take their toll, tables and indexes can become fragmented to the point where accessing them in their fragmented state degrades response time.

- **SQL Query Combination Traffic** – Nearly all SQL queries are written and tuned in a vacuum, meaning they're written, issued, and optimized one by one during the development phase of a database/application. The process is sometimes deceptive. A well-optimized query may run extremely quickly when issued by itself, but that same query's speed may slow to a crawl when it is executed alongside other queries that access the same objects.

- **Increased Data Volume** – Saving the most common for last, this performance vampire plagues nearly every dynamic database. Stories are legion where a database that performed exceedingly well with moderate data volumes becomes a sloth when the database size increased dramatically or built up slowly over time.

While looking over the various showstoppers and performance vampires mentioned above, the thought that likely occurs is "How in the world can one account and plan for such things?" Without question, such a task can be incredibly difficult to accomplish, especially when attempted through traditional manual processes. It used to be that all applications were put through a model office or testing phase before they were rolled out into production. The plan was that this transitional period would flush out any obvious application and database bugs and provide an indicator of how the system would perform on the first day of production.

This process can succeed for small applications, but for larger, enterprise-wide systems, the practice breaks down for a number of reasons. The most obvious flaw is that the end-user test bed can be woefully inadequate for pushing a database and its accompanying application hard enough.

What traditionally happens is that a handful of users are typically called upon to test a system that will eventually service hundreds or thousands of users. During the testing period, some performance issues may be uncovered and averted for production, but many of the showstopper and performance vampire issues previously listed will be overlooked and will remain in the database like a time bomb waiting to go off.

When the first day of production rolls around and the database goes live, things quickly turn ugly. The results are one or more days of constant fire drills for the database staff as they work to remedy the emergencies that have resulted from real-world stress placed on the database. This same set of circumstances can happen to an existing system when application consolidations or mergers occur and a wave of new users and demands come flooding in to what used to be a well-running database.

What can be done to make sure this doesn't happen? How can the ticking time bombs in the database be located and addressed? How can the database professional reach a level of confidence that performance will be excellent no matter what stress is eventually introduced into the database? Performance testing is the simple answer to each of these questions.

Performance Testing to the Rescue

Proper performance testing catches the showstopper and performance vampire problems that inadequate user and quality assurance testing can miss. In a nutshell, performance testing simulates what is expected from real world use. It stresses the database in ways that could otherwise only be accomplished by opening the floodgates to the production user community.

Smart performance testing uses the following elements to pull off a realistic simulation of what a database will experience during expected production usage:

- **Anticipated User Presence** – It is critical that the test simulate the number of user connections that are expected during peak times as well as normal working hours. This is the major area where manual testing methods that pick a subset of users to test a database/application experience failure. The database may run fine with 15 or so user connections, but may fail when 300 connect to the system.

- **Repetitive User Activity** – Once the anticipated user sessions have connected to the database, they obviously have to do something for the system to be stressed. To test effectively, they can't just "do something" once. Either all or a portion of the connected sessions need to repetitively perform tasks as they would during a normal workday. For an OLTP system, this may mean entering multiple orders. For a data warehouse, this may mean issuing long running analytical queries. The key is that the work is recurring so repeated blows are dealt against the database.

- **Extended Duration** - Once there are a set number of sessions performing repetitive work, ensure that the work continues for a period of time to make the test meaningful. Performing this test should unearth problems that take time to develop. For example, a SQL Server table may not become fragmented after 30 minutes of OLTP work, but may surprisingly fragment in a dramatic fashion after two or more hours of repeated action.

- **Expected Production Data Volume** – In order to have a truly valid test, the database should be loaded with test data that is approximately the size the database is expected to be in a year or so.

How can performance testing address both the hit-the-wall problems and the silent killers of database performance? How should the test be arranged to flush out all the major headaches that threaten the database? The next section will address these questions.

Addressing Showstopper Problems with Performance Testing

How can performance testing be used to bring database showstopper problems to light? A good beginning is to follow these general guidelines:

- **Testing Space Outages**: These problems typically rear their heads in dynamic OLTP environments in which data is constantly being added and changed. However, data warehouses can encounter space issues as well during periodic warehouse updates and refreshes. Performance testing can simulate database Data Manipulation Language (DML) activities such as INSERT, UPDATE and DELETE by repetitively executing SQL statements or stored procedures that either add data in a general fashion to one or more database objects or follow a more transactional process and add data throughout related database objects. For the latter, stored procedure executions work best.

- **Testing the Reaching of Resource Limits**: Certain resource limits can be tested merely by simulating the logging on of hundreds of user accounts (database process/session limits, etc.) Other limit tests require challenges similar to having those hundreds of sessions issue a query at the same time.

- **Testing Lock Contention**: The task of simulating potential locking problems can be easy or difficult depending on the underlying application design. The best way to accomplish this is to have simulated sessions repetitively executing database stored procedure logic that performs transactional work (DML activity).

Addressing Performance Draining Problems with Performance Testing

What about properly testing performance inefficiencies that can only appear with a sufficient load being introduced to the database? How about problems that take time to develop? There are practical ways to carry out these tests such as:

- **Testing I/O and File Contention**: This can only be done well when the expected numbers of concurrently connected sessions are brought against the database *and* those sessions are performing repetitive examples of transactional or query work. Duration may or may not play a role in flushing out problems in this area.

- **Testing CPU and Memory Exhaustion**: As with testing I/O, a full user load performing real work will tell the tale. Sometimes, however, just creating sessions on the database will bring memory problems to light as each session consumes memory even when idle. Other specific database-related memory metrics, such as cache hit ratios, etc., can only be evaluated through repetitive and consistent pressure from query activity.

- **Testing Database Object Fragmentation**: This process can be greatly accelerated by imposing a DML load on the database over a short duration of time that is heavier than the system would normally take weeks or months to accomplish. The goal is to determine if wasted space, row chaining/forwarding, extended index depths, etc., results from heavy INSERT, UPDATE, and DELETE activity.

- **Testing SQL Query Combination Traffic**: This task is somewhat more difficult in that a baseline of various SQL queries on a standalone basis needs to be acquired. Those baselines must then be compared against their per execution measures when they are introduced to a database in combination.

- **Testing Production Data Volume**: Loading a database with a representative data volume can be difficult if there is not a current system to pull it from. There are, however, data generators on the market that can help with this task.

Build or Buy?

Even database professionals who understand the need for real world testing of their databases and know what areas need to be stressed are often at a loss for the practical creation of the scenarios they need for pulling off a true performance test. This is not surprising when one considers all the manual work that has to go into such an effort for it to yield the answers that will give the Go/No Go signal to a database project team. It is often much easier to perform a small test with a select group of willing users and then hope that all goes well on the first day of production or when a massive upgrade begins.

This does not have to be the case. On the market, performance testing solutions exist that are designed to bring peace of mind to a database staff by allowing them to know which areas of a database will break prior to it going into production or experiencing a large upgrade. By simulating production or accelerated user and data volume, these products can make the database unbreakable by revealing the weaknesses of the database before users find them. The end result is ironclad availability and performance for the production systems. Examples include simple and inexpensive products like the SQL/Database Hammer from the SQL Server 2000 resource kit, and more robust, but pricier, products like Mercury's LoadRunner and Embarcadero Technologies' Extreme Test.

It is certainly possible to build robust testing solutions in-house; although, the manual effort that goes into creating and maintaining them can be prohibitive. Whether a company is choosing to purchase software to manage testing or deciding to custom build such a solution, someone must make sure that the system adheres to the previously detailed guidelines in order to be successful.

The Link between Change Control and Performance

Very few DBAs consider the effects that change control has on the performance of their SQL Server systems. If there is any doubt that a change control is needed to protect the database from performance problems, the following true story should be considered.

A seasoned DBA, who was managing a large packaged financial application, had to make a complex change to one of the database's critical tables. She thought she had built the right script to do the job. Unfortunately, she did not have everything in place, and when she ran her change job, she ended up losing a number of important indexes that existed on the table.

Worse yet, since her table and data looked okay, she thought all was well and did not know that the necessary indexes were lost. This is easy to do, especially with today's financial packages that have thousands of objects. The next day, many parts of the application slowed down to a crawl as queries that used to complete in an instant had started taking forever.

The changed table was identified as the source of the problem, but while the DBA discovered that the table now had no indexes, she did not know which columns had been indexed. Again, this is not uncommon in huge financial applications. Through trial and error, she was able to get her indexing scheme back in place, but not before a lot of time had been lost.

This is a good example of where good change control can save time and headaches. If the DBA is smart and deploys a good change control tool in the environment, she is pretty well set to recover from such a problem. Nearly every good tool in this category offers a synchronization feature that allows a DBA to compare an up-and-running database with a saved snapshot of that database's object definitions. Once differences are identified, a click of the mouse can restore any missing objects.

A change control tool can also help in physical design iterations. By periodically capturing changes made to the physical design of the database, it can be revealed what worked and what did not. And, if a mistake occurs and actually causes harm, the change control tool can be instructed to automatically put things back the way they were.

Now, if a company does not have the budget to purchase such a tool, it may be possible to get by with taking periodic SQL extractions using the Microsoft supplied tools, but this approach tends to fall short of what is really needed for good change control.

The fact is that change control protects the DBA in ways that traditional backup and recovery plans do not. The basics of change management for SQL Server revolve around the following four activities:

- **Database/Schema Archiving**: This is not to be confused with data archiving in which lesser-used data is moved to other databases/servers so performance on the primary server is increased. Instead, this concerns taking snapshots of database security, configuration, and data/code object definitions to preserve what the database looked like at a particular point in time.

- **Database Comparison**: Every SQL Server DBA has asked or been asked the question "What Changed?" countless times. Change management allows the DBA to intelligently answer this question through the use of smart comparisons between live SQL Server databases or archived definitions of SQL Server databases.

- **Database Migration**: Copying or cloning all or parts of a SQL Server database can be challenging given certain environments. Change management provides ways for intelligent full or partial copies of databases to be carried out without worry. This is one of the only areas Microsoft supplied tools can be of help.

- **Database Synchronization**: Synchronization is generally performed for one of two reasons: when unwanted definition, configuration, or security changes occur to a database, a DBA will want to roll back to a particular point in time or a DBA applies definition changes to one database that they want propagated to other databases.

The bulk of SQL Server performance is obtained through smart physical design, so everything that can be done to protect that design should be implemented, and this means setting up a good change control system and process.

As with nearly every other DBA process, it is best to use automation as much as possible so that things above routine housekeeping activities can be concentrated on. This being the case, schedule and automate the snapshot of key databases so they, like backup routines, are handled automatically.

The database/schema archives should be treated with the same care given to the backup files, so the DBA should make sure any archives are picked up by system wide backup jobs that run in the environment. If there are complex database schemas, with lots of objects, archive snapshots should be taken in off hours to avoid any resource hits on the server during prime time work hours, as heavy duty Data Definition Language extraction can be expensive.

Conclusion

This first phase of performance lifecycle management is by far the most important step in the PLM cycle. A strong and proper physical design lays the foundation for everything that follows in a database:

- A project should never be compromised by neglecting the database's physical design phase.

- Much of a database's performance comes from its physical design foundation.

- When troubleshooting system performance, an eye should be kept on indicators that signal a problem with the overall database physical design.

Good performance testing validates the physical design implementation and provides the confidence needed when a new production system goes live:

- Proper performance testing catches the showstopper and performance vampire problems that inadequate user and quality assurance testing miss.

- Performance testing simulates what is expected from real world use.

Finally, an automated change control process protects the physical design and serves as a key safety net for the database's foundation:

- The presence of a good change control tool in the environment can aid in a recovery process.

- A change control tool may offer a synchronization feature that allows a DBA to compare an up-and-running database with a saved snapshot of that database's object definitions.

- A change control tool can also help in physical design iterations. If a mistake has been made, this tool can be instructed to automatically put things back as they were.

The next chapter will explain phase two of PLM, which deals with the establishment of intelligent monitoring plans that keep the DBA informed of how well the physical design is working to meet the demanding needs of the applications that rely on it for service.

Performance Lifecycle Management - Step Two

The second step in Performance Lifecycle Management (PLM) involves proactive performance testing.

Establishing a Smart Monitoring Plan

The goals of a successful SQL Server Performance Monitoring Plan include the following:

- **Stop Unwanted Downtime:** Naturally, key database servers must be kept available for use by the business systems that need access to data.

- **Reduce Time to Detect and Resolve Performance Problems:** Some businesses have the potential to lose tens of thousands of dollars per hour when a database is down or in trouble. Therefore, it is critically important that a staff is able to restore a database to peak performance in the shortest amount of time possible.

- **Proactively Remove Threats to Key Databases:** It is much better to detect that a SQL Server transaction log is 70% full and take action rather than waiting for it to be 100% full and denying transactions from completing.

- **Increase Staff Knowledge and Productivity:** Database opinion polls routinely state that a DBA spends anywhere from 27-44% of their time monitoring and troubleshooting database systems. Data center managers need their staff to be fully educated and up-to-speed on the best database troubleshooting techniques available so they can quickly resolve performance issues and move on to more strategic tasks.

To help troubleshoot and optimize the performance of today's complex SQL Server systems, database professionals either build homegrown scripts or turn to software that is designed to monitor the activity of a busy system. The goal of either approach is to smartly present statistical data in a meaningful way so that the DBA or developer can confirm acceptable availability and performance, or recognize a potential threat as far in advance as possible and take action.

A global, smart performance plan will include the following three forms of monitoring:

- Cursory Real Time
- Analytic Real Time
- 24 X 7, unattended around-the-clock

Within each of these monitoring forms, three styles of analysis will need to be employed. They are as follows:

- Bottleneck
- Workload
- Ratio

This chapter will provide a summary of each monitoring form as well as a quick synopsis of each monitoring methodology. Upcoming chapters will dive deeper into each analysis methodology and show how to accurately monitor SQL Servers across the three monitoring forms.

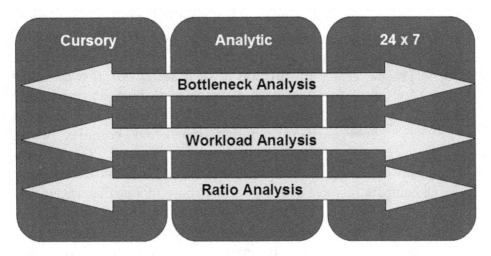

Figure 4.1: *Depiction of the three monitoring forms and analysis methods.*

General Monitoring Requirements

Regardless of the type of database monitor chosen, script-based, vendor supplied, etc., there are basic features that any good monitor should have. While more general features could be listed here, the most common features include:

- Past and Present DBMS Support.

- Ease of Navigation.

- Integration with Database Administration Software.

- Cross-Platform Capability.

Even if a company has standardized on a particular database platform, it is a sure bet that they will have multiple versions of that database running. Sometimes applications require an earlier version of a database since application vendors are notoriously slow at updating DBMS version support, while new development projects may be using the latest and greatest DBMS version. A good database monitor should at least support the versions of a database that the DBMS vendor themselves officially support.

 When a critical database problem presents itself, DBAs cannot waste time trying to figure out how to navigate through a chaotic, statistical maze of information in their search for answers. Instead, they need to have a product or system at their disposal that is easy to navigate and smartly leads them through the often complex world of database performance metrics. Good statistical organization, intelligent data presentations, and intuitive drill down views are all hallmark features of any good database monitoring system.

When people see the product integration point of a database monitor, they think of being able to invoke a monitor from some sort of administration console. This is certainly a desirable feature; however, it only takes the database professional halfway through the performance optimization process. If a database monitor points out a particular problem but offers no resolution capabilities, the DBA must manually proceed on their own.

Complete integration means that not only can a database monitor be invoked from an administration console, but that the monitor also integrates back into the console's facility to help fix any identified problem. As an example, if a database monitor identifies a space shortage in an SQL Server database, the DBA should be able to highlight the problem database in the monitor, click an integration link in the tool, and be placed into an administration console at the appropriate editor or utility needed to correct the problem. Auto-correction mechanisms requiring no human intervention are also an option, but are best left to 24 x 7 style monitors.

The need for cross-platform capability depends, of course, on whether a company uses a database platform other than the SQL Server. Such a need also depends on the dynamics of a company, as some large companies may have business units that use more than one RDBMS platform, while other units rely on only one database engine.

In general, it is a good thing to have a database monitor that offers cross-platform capabilities as one tool can offer the benefit of having just one interface to learn, which equates to a reduced learning curve for those needing to monitor multiple platforms.

The next three sections will present the different monitoring safety nets and will reveal what is involved with each one.

Cursory Monitoring

The most practiced form of monitoring in the SQL Server and every other database engine is probably cursory monitoring. This is a quick-hit, light survey of the activities that are currently in progress on the SQL Server, with the goal being to gain a basic understanding of what is going on and to take action on any obvious problems that are noticed.

Once it has been determined that the SQL Server is actually available, there are three basic sets of performance data that are of interest:

- Session traffic, along with each session's associated resource usage data.

- SQL currently being executed.

- Global database and O/S performance metrics.

In general, the goal is to determine who is logged on to the SQL Server, what SQL each session is currently running, and a global picture of resource usage on the server. For the SQL Server, this data is very easy to come by.

If using personal performance scripts and not a third party or Microsoft's supplied base database monitor, a user will discover that a quick combination of data dictionary views and one DataBase Consistency Check (DBCC) can get what is needed. Session information can be acquired by querying the *master..sysprocesses* table, with each session's currently executing SQL being obtained via the DBCC INPUTBUFFER(SESSION ID) command. Global SQL Server

---

performance statistics can be viewed by querying the *master..sysperfinfo* table.

SQL Server 2005 also provides a number of new monitoring views, which are all prefaced with *dm_* for dynamic management, in the *master* database. Upcoming chapters will provide a number of good scripts that can be used to view all of this information. Operating system metrics are not easily queried via SQL commands, but they can be viewed by using a Windows supplied performance monitor as well as getting a few O/S statistics via the new SQL Server 2005 views.

Cursory-style monitoring should not be relied on solely as there are some drawbacks such as:

- Data is cumulative only, which can be deceiving. Delta statistics are often better measures of current database performance. Examples include metrics like physical reads, full scans, etc.

- Data is in real time only, with no history being available for more analysis.

- Lack of deep drill downs means locating intricate performance nuances is impossible.

- No monitoring coverage when application is left unattended.

- Little assistance is offered in finding problems through statistical organization or visual identifiers.

- No threshold capabilities to signal performance exceptions.

- No alerting mechanisms such as paging, email, SNMP, etc. are available.

- No ability to get global handles on SQL statement execution patterns.

When cursory level monitoring fails to uncover server performance issues, the DBA has to then move on to a deeper form of monitoring known as analytic real time monitoring.

Analytic Real Time Monitoring

Analytic monitoring differs from a cursory approach in a number of respects. It involves more subject areas than cursory. The basic monitoring categories reviewed are:

- Memory
- I/O
- Space
- User Activity
- SQL Execution
- Ancillary, including replication, jobs, error log analysis, etc.

Even though this form of monitoring traditionally does not employ agents to collect statistics, the DBA still has the ability to get down to a fine grain of detail. The SQL Server architecture makes it pretty easy to collect this type of detail without agents, which is nice. The extended stored procedures presented in the Microsoft engine allows quite a bit of data to be acquired, and the Windows O/S performance counters are pretty easy to come by too.

The key thing to keep in mind is the ability to get a good overview of performance and the ability to immediately recognize issues that need attention. Once potential problems are identified, the user can dive in deeper for an in-depth look at the details. For example, maybe there is a script that displays a number of key metrics, one of which is a count of the number of errors in the SQL Server error log for a particular day in question. If a non-zero output for the error log count is shown, the DBA should quickly jump in and see the actual error log line items for the day.

While analytic monitoring is more robust than cursory, it still suffers from some of the same drawbacks as cursory-style monitoring such as:

- Data is in real time only, with no history being available for more analysis; however, some analytic monitors do offer rudimentary forms of record and playback.

- No monitoring coverage when application is left unattended.

- No alerting mechanisms such as paging, email, SNMP, etc. are available.

- No automatic corrective actions fire when performance thresholds are crossed.

The next option involves around-the-clock monitoring.

24 x 7 Monitoring

Ad-hoc monitoring works great when used as intended, but it loses traction under certain circumstances. Certain critical databases require special attention, which normally equates, among other things, to around-the-clock supervision. Often, the sheer number of databases that require monitoring can present problems and require that a specialized set of monitoring software be used.

For these scenarios, an enterprise database monitor or homegrown process is needed. An enterprise monitoring setup is designed to manage the performance of 24 x 7 applications as well as handle the unique needs of large SQL Server database farms. With the features of cursory and intelligent client-side monitoring components, enterprise 24 x 7 monitoring will also sport these key capabilities:

- Provides constant, unattended monitoring of assigned databases.

- Offers scalability features for large database farms.

- Supplies proactive notification and correction mechanisms to minimize database downtime.

- Provides historical analysis of performance metrics.

To be truly effective for critical databases, a database monitoring system needs to be on duty at all times. This means the monitoring system needs to be working even when the database or operations staff is not. Such a capability implies functionality far beyond the graphical user interface (GUI) normally used for assessing the performance of a database.

The 24 x 7 monitoring system polls its assigned database without the use of any visual interface and enforces predefined limits in terms of what it will accept as proper activity. To avoid downtime and large performance dips, the enterprise monitoring system must offer robust notification and automated correction mechanisms that detect performance exceptions as far in advance as possible, notify responsible parties immediately, and take action when it is instructed to do so.

The sheer size of an SQL Server database installation can be a challenge in its own right. Traditional manual ad-hoc database monitoring breaks down when the number of staff members is greatly outpaced by the number of key databases that need monitoring. Only an automated scalable approach can be confidently used to guard the availability and performance of a large database installation.

When scalability is mentioned in the context of database monitoring, it can mean many different things. However, the following is a "must have" list of capabilities that have to be present in the enterprise monitoring system for it to be effective in terms of scale:

- **Handle Increasing Monitoring Load** – The monitoring system must be able to add, subtract, and handle assigned databases easily, while maintaining consistent operation.

- **Offer Intelligent Enterprise Views** – The monitoring system should provide ways to quickly summarize performance across all monitored databases, and should give an idea of what is up, what is down, and what needs attention. This is not an easy thing to do in many circumstances.

The next section reviews the pros and cons of buying a third-party monitoring package versus building one from scratch.

Build versus Buy

When it comes to cursory, analytic, and 24 x 7 monitoring many SQL Server performance analysts become confused over whether to buy a third party monitoring package or build a system from scratch. There are positives and negatives to each approach.

Buying a third party solution can work out well as long as the system's specific requirements are met. Cursory monitoring is usually supported quite well by any of the major database tools vendors, but it is also taken care of in Microsoft's own Enterprise Manager/Management Studio. Analytic monitoring is not accomplished very well with Microsoft's own tools, even in SQL Server 2005. There are, however, a number of good third party analytic monitors on the market that do support SQL Server quite well. Pulling the "buy" trigger on a 24 x 7 monitoring solution is the point when things can get confusing.

Some SQL Server professionals have succeeded at building a robust around-the-clock monitoring system from scratch, but they have done so at a cost of many man-hours. Such a system usually involves the configuration of a number of stored procedures that are launched via a scheduling tool, normally the SQL Agent. These procedures are tied to a number of alerts that can call more customized scripts that perform predefined corrective actions. And that's just for one server! The addition of other SQL Servers to the equation and things can get messy fast.

This is not to say that building an in-house enterprise monitoring system cannot be done, for there are plenty of installations that have them. The cost of building and maintaining such a system needs to be weighed. While it will not impact users financially from a line-item budget standpoint, they might spend more than first thought in other ways, such as man-hours for development and maintenance, when everything is said and done.

Regardless of whether a third-party solution is chosen or the decision is made to build the solution in-house, performance monitoring is essential. The following section will delve more deeply into performance monitoring methodologies.

Performance Methodologies

In most dynamic SQL Server environments, users will find themselves actively engaged in all three types of monitoring described above at one time or another. No matter what type of monitoring is in use, one of the three types of analysis or a mixture of each will be employed each time the SQL Server is interrogated. The next several chapters will contain detailed explanations of each type of analysis, along with performance scripts that can be put to work immediately in the environment. For now, the next section will briefly cover each performance methodology to show what should be expected.

Bottleneck Analysis

What is causing the SQL Server to wait? This is the question that bottleneck analysis is intended to answer. Many database gurus today agree that bottleneck analysis is the most important performance technique that SQL Server DBAs should use while troubleshooting servers experiencing response time issues. The reason is because it uncovers the major problem areas faster than other analytical practices.

The next two chapters cover this form of analysis in much greater detail, and highlight the four major areas that a DBA reviews when practicing bottleneck analysis:

- Storage
- System (overall engine)
- Sessions
- Operating System

Workload Analysis

Workload analysis focuses on session traffic and activity that occurs on a SQL Server. One logical area in which to focus review involves issued SQL statements and stored code like procedures and triggers. Whether it is one or more sessions or particular blocks of SQL code that are being analyzed, a DBA will use workload analysis to attempt to determine above average usage of resources, such as CPU, memory, I/O, etc., to ferret out activity levels that are commanding the majority of the SQL Server's attention.

Standard rules of thumb dictate that if a process or SQL code block that is eating up 25% or more of a particular area such as CPU is identified, and it is not part of a large batch job or another recognized process known for needing lots of resources at particular points in time, it needs to be investigated in detail.

Ratio Analysis

Ratios have gotten a bad reputation over the past few years with many database experts, especially those in the Oracle community, stating that most ratios are worthless in the evaluation of the overall efficiency of a database server. Without question, there is some merit to these claims as global, cumulative ratios can give the DBA a false sense of security and convey a rosy picture, when in reality, performance has taken a turn for the worse.

However, one should avoid throwing the good out with the bad when considering the use of ratios in performance analysis. There are still plenty of valid ratios in the SQL Server that certainly deserve attention. For example, if a particular table had 1,000 forwarded rows in it, would the DBA be able to tell whether the table needed to be reorganized? Probably not. But if the DBA was told that 95% of the rows in that same table were forwarded in nature, all the information needed to take action would be available. That is why ratios are still valuable to the DBA.

Microsoft has tweaked some of the ratio-based performance counters over the years to make them more valuable to SQL Server professionals. For example, the cache hit ratio value was somewhat useless to DBAs once a server had been up and running for several hours, because the metric is cumulative in nature. If a large flood of physical I/O activity swept in, it would not make a dent in the overall statistic because there was too much other I/O involved in the calculation that prohibited its intervention. Now, however, the SQL Server service packs have included changes that cause the cache hit ratio metric to take into account only the last few thousand page I/Os, which makes the statistic much more meaningful.

Conclusion

Smart SQL Server monitoring plans will include a mixture of cursory, analytic real time, and unattended 24 x 7 monitoring activities. Within each of these monitoring forms will be three analysis methods: bottleneck, workload, and ratio analysis. If these plans are executed properly, the DBA will need no other safety net to guard the availability and performance of their SQL Servers.

The next chapter begins the presentation of bottleneck analysis, and describes how to use this technique to uncover issues within the storage and system areas of SQL Server.

Bottleneck Analysis: Part One

Diagnosing Storage and System Problems

SQL Server performance analysis can be carried out in many ways, and it seems that every database professional has their own preferred method. The process of diagnosing performance issues is somewhat likened to investment/stock analysis. There are many techniques that investors use to choose stocks for their portfolios, but most techniques can be boiled down into two basic methods: fundamental analysis and technical analysis.

Those who follow the fundamental analysis approach look for things such as continuous increases in a company's earnings per share, sales and revenue growth rates, profit margins, and other key factors that typically indicate a company's stock may be ready to rise. Proponents of technical analysis sneer at fundamentalists and insist that the way to pick winning stocks is by examining chart patterns of a company's stock, along with other market-leading indicators that can signal when to buy or sell.

Even though both techniques have their advocates, there are some pretty good investment professionals who, instead of limiting themselves to one method, embrace both. The bursting of the tech bubble in the early 2000's taught technical enthusiasts one thing: a company's fundamentals and bottom line do matter. Fundamentalists also learned that even a stock with outstanding corporate sales and revenue acceleration could be dragged down when its peers in the same industry group decline.

To properly tackle SQL Server performance analysis, it is critical that one does not get pigeon-holed into a narrow way of thinking in terms of how to approach performance optimization. It is important to make sure that all bases are covered. The previous chapter introduced the three main performance methodologies, which are bottleneck, workload, and ratio analysis. This chapter focuses on the primary method of troubleshooting SQL Server performance issues; bottleneck analysis.

What is Bottleneck Analysis?

When the SQL Server is up and running, every connected process is either busy doing work or waiting to perform work. A process that is waiting may mean nothing in the overall scheme of things, or it can be an indicator that a database bottleneck exists.

This is when wait-based or bottleneck analysis comes into play. DBAs use this form of performance analysis to determine if perceived bottlenecks in a database are contributing to a performance problem.

Bottleneck analysis is a valid method of measuring performance because it helps a DBA track where a database server, user sessions, the operating system and etc., have been spending their time. If I/O completion waits or heavy table-scan activity has been dragging a database's performance down, a DBA can use bottleneck analysis to confirm the actual root cause.

Most likely, a DBA who has to manage Oracle databases in addition to the SQL Server is no stranger to bottleneck analysis. Oracle introduced a wait event interface long ago, although no one really began to notice it until Oracle7. As of this writing, Oracle Database 10g has been out for about a year, and if the DBA has migrated to it, it is likely that person has seen the increased emphasis Oracle has put on bottleneck analysis as the primary method to use in identifying performance issues.

SQL Server professionals are just now beginning to recognize the benefits of using a bottleneck approach to performance analysis. Much like the early days of Oracle, few SQL Server DBAs have looked at Microsoft's wait event interface, but this is beginning to change. There is more to bottleneck analysis than just examining wait events, called wait types in SQL Server. Broadly speaking, there are two major types of bottlenecks for which the DBA should be on the lookout.

The first type of bottleneck is the "hit the wall" variety. An example of this would be a SQL Server database running out of space in its transaction log or a database suddenly going offline. For all intents and purposes, work grinds to a complete stop, or the impact of the bottleneck is great enough to stop major activities. These types of bottlenecks, usually called immediate bottlenecks, are the kind that should be detected far in advance of their actual occurrence, because when they do occur, the DBA can expect the phone to immediately start ringing off the hook with users lodging complaints.

The second type of bottleneck is more insidious because it is gradual in nature. The bottleneck starts slowly with hardly anyone noticing a performance slowdown, but it begins to build in effect and intensity. It slowly starts to drain the life from the SQL Server system, and because of this, it has been nicknamed a vampire. An example of this type of bottleneck is similar to object fragmentation, in which an object becomes more and more disorganized until I/O performance is drastically affected.

When troubleshooting immediate and vampire styled bottlenecks, typically four areas of the SQL Server are reviewed:

- Storage
- System
- Sessions
- Operating System

This chapter will examine how to detect, diagnose, and resolve both immediate and vampire bottlenecks in the storage and system areas. The other two areas will be reserved for the next chapter.

Storage Bottlenecks

When it comes to understanding what SQL Server is doing underneath the covers with respect to space, Microsoft's engine actually is not as straightforward as some of the other database platforms. The ability to easily report database and transaction log space from a global perspective is not as simple or thorough as some administrators would like it to be.

Also, the *sp_spaceused* procedure used for object and database space does not really yield the whole space picture for an object or database. Diagnosing fragmentation problems in a database requires a fairly skilled hand with the ability to not only interpret a number of different object fragmentation metrics, but to also understand the environment and mechanics of the applications that use the database.

As with other database engines, SQL Server storage problems have the capability to immediately stop an otherwise well-running database and server completely in its tracks. Space problems also have the potential to slowly eat away at performance until response times become unbearably slow for a database community.

Since storage has such a powerful hold over a database, it is imperative that the DBA understand how SQL Server uses space, be equipped with the right tools/scripts and knowledge to proactively plan storage and object structures, and be able to quickly diagnose and fix space problems when they occur. To kick things off, a quick review of how the SQL Server is organized in terms of space, both at the database and object level is merited.

A Quick SQL Server Storage Primer

A database is the logical SQL Server container that holds user data and other necessary objects such as stored procedures. Beginning in SQL Server 7, Microsoft did away with the old Sybase device method of storage definitions and went to a cleaner implementation of one or more database files, which reside on the server. Each database begins life with a primary database file that is used to house system tables and other metadata, and a log file that is used for database recovery purposes. Other files may be created as well. The SQL Server database and log files have a fair amount of flexibility in terms of being increased or decreased in size.

The DBA can also make use of filegroups, which are collections of database files. Administrators can use filegroups to explicitly place objects for load balancing and performance purposes. Unfortunately, many DBAs do not smartly utilize filegroups, which is a shame because Microsoft has given the DBA even more flexibility in filegroup usage in SQL Server 2005 where table and index partitioning across filegroups, sometimes called *data_spaces* in 2005, is supported. Transaction log files are never members of filegroups, and a database file can only be a member of one filegroup.

Databases are comprised of logical pages, each of which is a fixed eight KB in size. The eight KB page is also a unit of I/O for the SQL Server, which affects performance and locking. The two fundamental units of database storage, the table and index, make use of pages to hold their information. There are also specialty database pages such as Global Allocation Map, Page Free Space, and Index Allocation Map, that are used for system management purposes.

As filegroups are collections of database files, extents are collections of database pages. An extent is made up of eight, eight KB pages and is therefore 64 KB in size. Extents come in two types, uniform and mixed. Uniform extents ascribe all eight database pages to a single object; whereas, mixed extents have the potential to hold multiple objects. With mixed extents, the SQL Server tries to preserve space by not allowing very small objects to take up an entire extent and therefore, waste a lot of space.

Before moving on to techniques for monitoring storage, a quick word on hardware storage and performance is in order.

A Coming Physical I/O Crisis?

A number of database experts are predicting a coming crisis with respect to database performance and disk I/O. This prediction has to do with the fact that hard disks are continually increasing in their ability to handle more storage capacity. The concern is that the I/O's per second (iops) that these disks can service has not kept pace with their ability to handle more space.

For example, a DBA used to have ten or more disks at their disposal to service the storage needs of a 500 GB database. But now, storage vendors can offer IT managers the ability to store the same amount of data on only two disks. Such a proposal is not only attractive to IT management, but it often appeals to system administrators as well because fewer disks normally mean less work and maintenance.

Such a situation can place a stranglehold on the DBA's database because the number of iops that such a disk configuration can handle is far below the iops capability of the previous ten disks.

Storage is typically priced by capacity and not by iops, so database gurus are sounding the alarm for all DBAs to hear; make sure their voice is heard when the storage configuration of the database server is being decided. If their opinions are not heard, the database may be robbed of performance because of poor disk purchasing decisions.

Storage Monitoring Basics

With a basic understanding of how SQL Server uses storage out of the way, attention can be turned to how one should monitor space in SQL Server to avoid immediate and vampire bottlenecks.

As has already been presented, a storage bottleneck can be an overwhelming event that can completely stop the operation of a database if it is severe enough. In SQL Server, a storage bottleneck normally takes one of four forms:

- Lack of free space in a database.

- Lack of free space in a database transaction log.

- Lack of free space on the server.

- One or multiple forms of fragmentation.

It is important that a DBA be able to quickly spot storage bottlenecks before they threaten a database's availability and also know to correct and proactively prevent bottlenecks from interrupting the key operations of a database. In online transaction processing (OLTP) environments, the threat of exhausting the available free space in a database during peak working hours is always present. This being the case, how can the DBA easily spot storage bottlenecks before they stop the operation of one or more of the key databases?

The *up_bn_storage_overview* procedure below provides an overview of the storage situation on an SQL Server, versions 7 - 2000. It provides overview sections that display a count of databases, filegroups, and files, along with amounts for total database and log used in MB. It then displays detailed information for every database on the server and breaks out space by database and log. Finally, it displays information regarding space utilization on the server's hard disks.

up_bn_storage_overview.sql

```
-- Script is available in the Online Code Depot
```

Figure 5.1 is a representation of the results of the above script.

	database_count
1	7

	file_count
1	14

	file_group_count
1	14

	Total Database	Total Log
1	268.94	270.06

	database_name	total_log_space	log_can_grow	total_log_space_used	total_free_log_space	percent_log_used
1	er	157.31	Yes	62.12	95.19	39.49
2	er2	100.00	Yes	25.84	74.16	25.84
3	gim	10.00	Yes	2.66	7.34	26.63
4	master	.75	Yes	.44	.31	58.82
5	model	.50	Yes	.37	.13	73.61
6	msdb	.75	Yes	.43	.32	57.76
7	tempdb	.75	Yes	.41	.34	54.08

	database_name	total_space	total_db_space	db_can_grow	total_space_used	total_db_space_used	total_free_space	total_f
1	er	257.31	100.00	Yes	101.00	38.88	156.31	61.12
2	er2	200.00	100.00	Yes	57.34	31.50	142.66	68.50
3	gim	60.00	50.00	Yes	8.33	5.67	51.67	44.33
4	master	14.06	13.31	Yes	13.34	12.90	.72	.41
5	model	1.13	.63	Yes	.89	.52	.24	.11

Figure 5.1: *Output from the database server storage overview procedure.*

Before examining the procedure's output, a couple of notes about the SQL procedures and code that are shown in this book should be explained.

One will see a number of cursors used throughout most every procedure that builds constructs of tables and databases. It is certainly OK to replace them with the *sp_msforeachtable* and *sp_foreachdb* procedures that allow easy looping through table and database lists.

Sometimes it is necessary to show alternative procedures or queries for different versions of SQL Server because they vary too much to simply point out the distinctions. Other times, only one or more differences will be pointed out so the entire procedure's code will not have to be repeated.

In the case of the *up_bn_storage_overview* procedure, there is one query change that must be made for it to work on SQL Server 2005. Microsoft has deprecated the *sysindexes* table in favor of a number of new object/space tables that support new features such as partitioning. This being the case, the database space query in the above procedure will need to be replaced with the following code snippet:

🖫 up_bn_storage_overview (database space segment)

```
-- Script is available in the Online Code Depot
```

As the output from the *up_bn_storage_overview* procedure is examined, one will be able to see how the procedure helps to diagnose any immediate storage bottlenecks that are either current or on the verge of causing a problem. In the log and database details sections, columns for total, used, free, and free space percents, among other things, can be found. High percentage values in the percent used columns could indicate a potential immediate bottleneck brewing, but this is not always the case. There are a number of factors that need to be considered.

If the database is not dynamic in nature, meaning no data is being added or changed, a high percent used is actually desirable. Smart DBAs will size non-dynamic databases in a way that they are almost completely full so space is not wasted.

Perhaps the database has been configured to automatically grow in size when more space is required. This can be done by setting up one or more of the database's files to automatically extend in size when a request for more database space exceeds the amount of available free space. If this is the case, SQL Server will simply allocate more space when the need arises, provided no roadblocks are encountered. To see if the database has one or more files set for autogrowth, the *db_can_grow* and *log_can_grow* columns in the output can be checked. They will show if the database can extend to meet any critical space requests.

Setting autogrowth for a database and/or log, however, does not mean the DBA is home free in terms of avoiding a free space deficit. One must also ensure that the underlying database files will not encounter any space growth limitations and the database server has plentiful free space at the operating system level. The latter can be determined by checking the last section in the stored procedure's output as it will contain that information. In terms of database files hitting their maximum file size limit, a procedure will be provided later in this chapter to give that information.

Avoiding Free Space Deficit Bottlenecks

An SQL Server administrator will want to prevent all database free space deficits from occurring and will also want to know how to quickly fix a space deficit if one does indeed crop up. What sort of strategy and tactics should be used?

In terms of proactive actions, it is a good idea to have autogrowth turned on for dynamically growing databases. This puts the burden on the SQL Server's back in terms of ensuring free space deficits do not occur for the database. If any of the databases do not have autogrowth set, this can easily be changed by altering the database and setting the *filegrowth* and *maxsize* properties for one or more files.

If the phone is ringing with reports of a space outage, there are a couple of things that can be done quickly to rectify the situation. The autogrowth for the problem database can be enabled, allowing the SQL Server to take control. Or, one or more database/log files can be permanently enlarged by altering the *modify file* clause, which allows the file size to be dynamically changed providing there is enough free space on the disk. If a space deficit at the server level prevents this action, a new file on a different drive can be added to the database and the database enlarged in that fashion.

Autogrowth should not be used as a replacement for properly sizing a database. Each time the SQL Server enlarges a database file, a small performance penalty will be encountered, so it is wise to allocate the proper amount of space in the beginning.

While a simple query is not available to determine if data files are expanding, the following query can be used to check on any dynamic log file extensions:

🖫 log_expand.sql

```
-- Script is available in the Online Code Depot
```

In addition to applying all the principles discussed for preventing database free space deficits, there are a couple of other options available for database transaction logs.

If point-in-time recovery is not necessary for a database, the truncate log on the checkpoint option or simple recovery mode can be enabled. This tells SQL Server to flush the log of any committed transactions when a checkpoint is performed. Enabling this option is not a perfect safety net because a single long running transaction can still cause a log to fill completely up, since the truncate only flushes committed work.

If point-in-time recovery is needed for the databases, the smartest thing is to put a log backup maintenance plan in place that periodically backs up and truncates the log. This course of action provides good recovery capability for the database and depending on the backup frequency can help stop log free space deficits.

Server-Level Space Considerations

In terms of avoiding space deficits at the physical disk layer, the best preventative measure is to buy liberal amounts of disk space in the beginning. From an SQL Server standpoint, server free space deficits can be prevented by placing database and log files on lesser utilized drives. Drives that contain the operating system software and any swap files should be avoided.

From a performance standpoint, disks or arrays that exceed 80% of their capacity should be avoided. The New Technology File System (NTFS) needs room for its various house-keeping tasks to work, and when disks exceed 80% capacity, NTFS become less efficient, with the end result being impaired I/O.

The disk can be thought of in zones: inner, mid and outer. The bits in the inner zone move past the head much slower than the bits in the outer zone. Disks are engineered to write bits to the inner zone last, because I/O to that zone is up to four times slower. Thus, filling a disk beyond 80% capacity can result in slower performance as the system does I/O in that inner zone.

If it is noticed that there is over-allocated space for some of the databases, transaction logs, or files, the entire databases or individual files can be reduced in size with the DBCC SHRINKDATABASE or DBCC SHRINKFILE commands. There are various restrictions as to what the SQL Server can and cannot do with respect to shrinking databases and files, so the Microsoft online books should be consulted for a thorough presentation of the subject.

Before leaving the topic of general space monitoring, there is one oddity that needs to be highlighted regarding SQL Server space reporting. SQL Server does not consistently maintain space information in its internal tables and occasionally, both external storage-related queries and SQL Server's own space procedures will report invalid or negative values for space. If this occurs for any of the databases, the DBCC UPDATEUSAGE command can be run against the problem databases and the inaccuracies should disappear.

More Space Demographic Diagnostics

After checking the global storage picture of the SQL Server, one can then drill down to obtain more detail on filegroups, files and databases. The *up_bn_storage_filegroups* procedure will give some good information on the filegroup front:

🖫 **up_bn_storage_filegroups**

```
-- Script is available in the Online Code Depot
```

Figure 5.2 is a representation of the filegroup demographic information.

dbname	filegroupid	file_group	can_grow	file_count	size_in_mb	table_reserved_mb	index_reserved_mb	free_space_mb	free
er	0	LOG	YES	1	157.31	.00	.00	95.19	60.5
er	1	PRIMARY	YES	1	100.00	37.97	.91	61.12	61.1
er2	0	LOG	YES	1	100.00	.00	.00	74.16	74.1
er2	1	PRIMARY	YES	1	100.00	30.81	.69	68.50	68.5
gim	0	LOG	YES	1	10.00	.00	.00	7.34	73.3
gim	1	PRIMARY	YES	1	50.00	3.58	2.09	44.33	88.6
master	0	LOG	YES	1	.75	.00	.00	.30	39.7
master	1	PRIMARY	YES	1	13.31	12.64	.26	.41	3.08
model	0	LOG	YES	1	.50	.00	.00	.13	26.3
model	1	PRIMARY	YES	1	.63	.39	.13	.11	17.4
msdb	0	LOG	YES	1	.75	.00	.00	.32	42.2
msdb	1	PRIMARY	YES	1	3.00	2.60	.25	.15	5.00
tempdb	0	LOG	YES	1	.75	.00	.00	.31	41.7
tempdb	1	PRIMARY	YES	1	2.00	.45	.13	1.42	71.0

Figure 5.2: *Filegroup demographic information.*

The above procedure works well for SQL Server 7 – 2000. For SQL Server 2005, a change in the query that obtains object space totals for each filegroup will have to be made. This is because of the deprecation of the *sysindexes* table and the fact that partitioned objects are now supported:

⊞ up_bn_storage_filegroups (object space totals segment)
```
-- Script is available in the Online Code Depot
```

From filegroups, the DBA can drill down to the individual file level with the *up_bn_storage_files* procedure in SQL Server 2000 and above. This script will reveal whether any files are not enabled for autogrowth and if any file has a maximum file limit imposed.

⊞ up_bn_storage_files
```
-- Script is available in the Online Code Depot
```

Figure 5.3 is a representation of the demographic information for the database and log files.

dbname	logicname	file_group	filename	size_in_mb	can_grow	growth_amount	max_file_size_mb
er	erdata	PRIMARY	C:\Program Files\Microsoft SQL Server\MSSQL\erdata.mdf	100.00	YES	10%	UNLIMITED
er	erlog	LOG	C:\Program Files\Microsoft SQL Server\MSSQL\erlog.ldf	157.31	YES	10%	UNLIMITED
er2	erdata	PRIMARY	C:\Program Files\Microsoft SQL Server\MSSQL\er2.mdf	100.00	YES	10%	UNLIMITED
er2	erlog	LOG	C:\Program Files\Microsoft SQL Server\MSSQL\er2log.ldf	100.00	YES	10%	UNLIMITED
gim	gimdata	PRIMARY	C:\Program Files\Microsoft SQL Server\MSSQL\gimdata.mdf	50.00	YES	10%	UNLIMITED
gim	gimlog	LOG	C:\Program Files\Microsoft SQL Server\MSSQL\gimlog.ldf	10.00	YES	10%	UNLIMITED
master	master	PRIMARY	C:\Program Files\Microsoft SQL Server\MSSQL\Data\master.mdf	13.31	YES	10%	UNLIMITED
master	mastlog	LOG	C:\Program Files\Microsoft SQL Server\MSSQL\Data\mastlog.ldf	.75	YES	10%	UNLIMITED
model	modeldev	PRIMARY	C:\Program Files\Microsoft SQL Server\MSSQL\Data\model.mdf	.63	YES	10%	UNLIMITED
model	modellog	LOG	C:\Program Files\Microsoft SQL Server\MSSQL\Data\modellog.ldf	.50	YES	10%	UNLIMITED
msdb	MSDBData	PRIMARY	C:\Program Files\Microsoft SQL Server\MSSQL\Data\MSDBData.mdf	3.00	YES	0.25 MB	UNLIMITED
msdb	MSDBLog	LOG	C:\Program Files\Microsoft SQL Server\MSSQL\Data\MSDBLog.ldf	.75	YES	0.25 MB	UNLIMITED
tempdb	tempdev	PRIMARY	C:\Program Files\Microsoft SQL Server\MSSQL\Data\tempdb.mdf	2.00	YES	10%	UNLIMITED
tempdb	templog	LOG	C:\Program Files\Microsoft SQL Server\MSSQL\Data\templog.ldf	.75	YES	10%	UNLIMITED

Figure 5.3: *Demographic information for database and log files.*

For SQL Server 7 users, the filegroup and files procedures shown above can be used; however, the database cursor code will have to be altered to reference the proper database property function:

up_bn_storage_files (database cursor code segment)
```
-- Script is available in the Online Code Depot
```

If the intent is finding out if autogrowth is enabled for any of the databases or logs, or if any database or log is nearing its maximum file size limit, the *up_bn_storage_bnecks* procedure can be used. It gives a count of such issues along with detail on which database or logs have a problem on SQL Server can be used.

up_bn_storage_bnecks
```
-- Script is available in the Online Code Depot
```

Figure 5.4 is a representation of a listing of potential database and log bottlenecks.

A database_name	B can_db_grow	C can_log_grow	D can_db_shrink	E db_near_max_size	F log_near_max_size
er	Yes	Yes	No	No	No
er2	Yes	Yes	No	No	No
gim	Yes	Yes	No	No	No
master	Yes	Yes	No	No	No
msdb	Yes	Yes	No	No	No
tempdb	Yes	Yes	No	No	No

total_db_growth_problems	total_log_growth_problems	total_db_shrink_problems	total_db_maxsize_problems	total_log_maxsize_problems
0	0	0	0	0

Figure 5.4: *Uncovering potential database and log bottlenecks.*

With the introduction to immediate storage bottlenecks out of the way, attention can be turned to the vampire-styled bottleneck, which most often takes the form of object fragmentation in SQL Server.

Object Fragmentation

Plainly stated, the subject of SQL Server fragmentation is not that simple to handle. There are a variety of factors to consider when diagnosing fragmentation and contemplating the reorganization of database objects.

SQL Server fragmentation can be broken down into two basic types:

- **External Fragmentation:** This situation exists when indexes have a logical order, based on their key value, which does not match the actual physical order inside the database file that houses the index. When an ordered scan is performed on an index, I/O performance is enhanced when the physical order of the database pages matches the logical order of the index. This is because the disk head can scan in one direction instead of moving back and forth to obtain the needed information.

- **Internal Fragmentation:** This situation exists when tables and indexes are not utilizing space as efficiently as they should. The amount of wasted space in the database pages artificially inflates the size of the table or index and causes more I/O to be performed than would otherwise be needed if the object were compacted.

Fragmentation is not a performance factor once data reaches the SQL Server memory caches.

Environments That Benefit From Fragmentation Elimination

One important point regarding fragmentation is not every situation benefits from fragmentation removal. Before the DBA invests a considerable amount of time and effort into diagnosing and attempting the removal of fragmentation, it must first be determined whether jumping through hoops will actually improve the database's availability and performance.

At the highest level, the environments that benefit the most from fragmentation removal are read-intensive databases in which large indexes are being frequently scanned. There are a couple of reasons why this is the case.

In most OLTP environments, data retrieval tends to be mostly selective, which negates most of the bad effects of external fragmentation. OLTP environments also often benefit from internal fragmentation because it is smart to leave room on index pages that are being added to and updated frequently. Free index page space helps avoid the dreaded page split in which a page is divided in two due to the fact that incoming clustered index data cannot logically fit on a needed page, so the SQL Server makes room by creating two index pages out of one. Administrators oftentimes specify a low *fillfactor* for their indexes in order to create internal fragmentation and hopefully avoid page splits.

Data warehousing or databases with many resource-intensive/scanning queries are another matter. These environments will likely benefit from fragmentation removal. One reason is that the indexes tend to be larger, and therefore, are not cached by SQL Server as easily as small indexes. Fragmentation has no effect on performance once the data is nestled safely in SQL Server's memory caches.

Another reason why these environments benefit from fragmentation removal is the effect fragmentation has on SQL Server's read ahead manager. The read ahead manager helps queries that perform large scans by scanning index pages and data pages that it believes will be read and placing them into memory before they are actually needed. Naturally, this process can reduce overall scan times because data read in memory is many times faster than when that same data must be retrieved from disk.

However, fragmentation affects how well the read ahead manager works. The read ahead manager will dynamically adjust the size of I/O it performs based on the actual physical order of the data and index pages on the server. When little external fragmentation is present, the read ahead manager can work very efficiently because it can read larger blocks at a time; whereas, excessive fragmentation causes the read ahead manager to read smaller blocks of data. The end result when fragmentation is present is less overall throughput.

SQL execution patterns are something else to examine. Queries that perform large index scans are the ones that should see performance improvements when fragmentation is removed in a database.

Diagnosing Object Fragmentation

If there is an environment that will benefit from reducing fragmentation, how does the DBA go about rectifying the matter? There are a number of metrics and factors to consider before one can intelligently start creating reorganization plans.

 Prior to SQL Server 2005, Microsoft's main diagnostic weapon to help uncover object fragmentation was the DBCC SHOWCONTIG command. In SQL Server 7.0, the command is not easy to view for large numbers of objects because the output is very text-based. In SQL Server 2000 and higher, the command is easier to use in the DBCC. In SQL Server 2005, Microsoft has introduced a new function that makes it even simpler to query for fragmentation issues.

When using DBCC SHOWCONTIG to diagnose fragmentation in SQL Server 7 – 2000, particular attention should be paid to the following metrics:

- **Extent Scan Fragmentation:** This highlights any gaps or lack of contiguous order in extents and indicates the presence of external fragmentation. Percentages of 25-50% or more are not a favorable reading.

- **Logical Scan Fragmentation:** This metric represents the percentage of pages that are out of physical order. Values greater than 25% for this metric may mean that index scan performance is not what it could be. This statistic is meaningless for tables without clustered indexes (heap tables).

- **Average Page Density:** This metric represents the fullness of the data or index pages, and is an indicator of internal fragmentation. The more full a data or index page is, the less I/O needed by SQL Server when performing scans of tables or indexes. High values are good here, with anything below 50% being suspect. Low values for this metric often indicate the presence of page splitting. Internal fragmentation is not necessarily bad in OLTP environments where large *fillfactors* are often specified. Also, small objects, those will little or no data, will likely show low readings because they simply do not consume enough space in a database page. These objects can be ignored.

- **Extent Switches:** In a perfect world, this will equal the number of object extents minus one. Higher values, many times higher than an object's extent count, can indicate external fragmentation.

- **Scan Density:** This is computed by dividing the optimum number of extent switches by the actual number of extent switches. This percentage can be misleading, however, if the object spans more than one database file and should not be considered in such an event. Values close to 100% are best.

In SQL Server 2005, a new function called *sys.dm_db_index_physical_stat*s is available for use in diagnosing index fragmentation. More information regarding how this new function call is used later, but the following are the output columns from the function on which focus should be placed:

- **avg_fragmentation_in_percent:** the logical fragmentation percentage, which takes into account multiple files. Microsoft's rule of thumb is that any index with a score over 30 is a candidate for a rebuild/reorganization.

- **fragment_count:** the number of physically consecutive leaf pages in the index.

- **page_count:** number of data pages.

- **avg_page_space_usec_in_percent:** describes how full the pages in the table/index are.

- **avg_fragment_size_in_pages:** the average number of pages in one fragment of the index. Larger numbers are better here.

As seen above, the DBA cannot just blindly diagnose fragmentation in the SQL Server, but instead needs to evaluate a number of individual metrics.

Object Fragmentation Diagnostic Procedures

The diagnostic scripts that the DBA will need to run will vary quite a bit, depending on the version of the SQL Server that is being used. For SQL Server version 7.0, the *up_bn_storage_tablediag7* and *up_bn_storage_indexdiag7* procedures should be used:

🖫 up_bn_storage_tablediag7
```
-- Script is available in the Online Code Depot
```

🖫 up_bn_storage_indexdiag7
```
-- Script is available in the Online Code Depot
```

For SQL Server version 2000, use the *up_bn_storage_tablediag8* and *up_bn_storage_indexdiag8* procedures:

🖫 up_bn_storage_tablediag8
```
-- Script is available in the Online Code Depot
```

🖫 up_bn_storage_indexdiag8

Figure 5.5 is a representation of a portion of index fragmentation diagnostics for SQL Server 2000.

owner	table_name	index_name	file_group	is_clustered	ExtentFrag	ScanDensity	AvgPageDensity	LogicalFrag	MinRecSize	MaxRecSize	Av
dbo	ADMISSION	ADMISSION__04232004191520001	PRIMARY	No	0.00	100.00	94.24	25.00	18	18	
dbo	ADMISSION	ADMISSION_REF148	PRIMARY	No	50.00	50.00	94.24	0.00	18	18	
dbo	ADMISSION	ADMISSION_REF447	PRIMARY	No	0.00	50.00	94.24	0.00	18	18	
dbo	DOCTOR	PK9	PRIMARY	No	0.00	100.00	2.94	0.00	18	18	
dbo	DOCTOR	robidx	PRIMARY	No	0.00	100.00	5.10	0.00	30	36	
dbo	DOCTOR_PROCEDURE	PK10	PRIMARY	No	0.00	50.00	88.00	0.00	36	36	
dbo	DOCTOR_PROCEDURE	REF623	PRIMARY	No	0.00	100.00	67.15	0.00	27	27	
dbo	DOCTOR_PROCEDURE	REF922	PRIMARY	No	0.00	100.00	92.64	0.00	18	18	
dbo	eas_collection	eas_collection_pk	PRIMARY	Yes	0.00	100.00	1.94	0.00	76	79	
dbo	eas_collection	eas_collection_fk1	PRIMARY	No	0.00	100.00	0.25	0.00	9	9	
dbo	eas_collection	eas_collection_fk2	PRIMARY	No	0.00	100.00	0.32	0.00	12	12	
dbo	eas_collection_object	eas_collection_object_uk	PRIMARY	Yes	0.00	100.00	54.20	0.00	19	19	
dbo	eas_collection_object	eas_collection_object_fk1	PRIMARY	No	0.00	100.00	28.38	0.00	9	9	
dbo	eas_collection_object	eas_collection_object_fk2	PRIMARY	No	0.00	100.00	28.38	0.00	9	9	
dbo	eas_collection_object	eas_collection_object_pk	PRIMARY	No	0.00	100.00	28.38	0.00	9	9	

Figure 5.5: *Example output of index fragmentation diagnostics for SQL Server 2000.*

The above procedures require a database name be passed, but it also allows the procedure's output to be filtered based on general filters like filegroup and object owner. They also allow the DBA to pass in fragmentation filter parameters so the output can be restricted to only objects that violate particular fragmentation thresholds.

In SQL Server 2005, it becomes pretty easy to get fragmentation metrics. The *sys.dm_db_index_physical_stats* function allows the DBA to use a simple SQL to view and filter out only the objects that need to be rebuilt. For example, to view all fragmentation statistics for all tables and indexes in a particular database, the following sample SQL can be used:

```
Select
*
from
sys.dm_db_index_physical_stats (default, '*', default, 'detailed')
go
```

Figure 5.6 shows a sample fragmentation output for SQL Server 2005.

	TableName	IndexName	PartitionNumber	IndexType	Depth	AvgFragmentation	Fragments	AvgFragmentSize	Pages	AvgPageFullness	Records	GhostRe
1	DEPT		1	Heap	1	0	0	0	1	7.596221	22	
2	DEPT		1	LOB Data	1	0	0	0	2	4.237707	8	
3	DOCTOR	DOCTOR_PK	1	Clustered Index	1	0	1	1	1	6.856931	12	
4	DOCTOR_PROCEDUR		1	Heap	1	0	0	0	3	71.01556	375	
5	EMBARCADERO_EXP		1	Heap	1	0	0	0	4	81.45849	170	
6	EMP		1	Heap	1	0	0	0	3520	99.4707	457848	
7	file_info		1	Heap	1	0	0	0	5	76.90835	37	
8	IOT_TEST		1	Heap	1	0	0	0	1	0.5883222	2	
9	MEDICATION		1	Heap	1	0	0	0	1	4.546578	14	
10	MEDICATION_DISP		1	Heap	1	0	0	0	4	80.28189	500	
11	MEDICATION_DISPM		1	Heap	1	0	0	0	1	0.7907091	3	
12	new_nurse		1	Heap	1	0	0	0	1	2.606889	4	
13	new_nurse		1	LOB Data	1	0	0	0	2	2.112676	4	
14	NURSE		1	Heap	1	0	0	0	1	3.99061	9	
15	NURSE_PROCEDURE		1	Heap	1	0	0	0	2	83.3704	375	
16	ORDERS		1	Heap	1	0	0	0	830	51.78595	830	
17	PATIENT		1	Heap	1	0	0	0	17	94.92382	1503	
18	PATIENT		1	LOB Data	1	0	0	0	20	76.82456	1503	
19	PATIENT_INSURANC		1	Heap	1	0	0	0	5	86.45911	500	
20	PATIENT_PR_042320		1	Heap	1	0	0	0	3	80.28169	375	
21	PATIENT_PROCEDUR		1	Heap	1	0	0	0	3	80.28169	375	

Figure 5.6: *Sample fragmentation output for SQL Server 2005.*

The *sys.dm_db_index_physical_stats* function allows the DBA to get information back for a whole database or just focus on a particular schema or table/index. The function can also be told whether to gather detailed statistics for the report, or just to use a limited or sample-based approach on gathering metrics. The latter two methods don't impose as strict a locking scheme during statistics gathering as detailed, so keep this in mind if concurrency is an issue.

A *where* clauses can also be used to restrict output of the function so back data on only those objects in need of a rebuild can be obtained.

Extent Proximity

Like many other database engines, SQL Server has a prefetch mechanism called the Read Ahead manager that will pull data into the memory caches it believes will be needed for operations such as full table scans. Having the data already present in memory ensures that response times are the shortest possible, so the Read Ahead capabilities are indeed good to have. However, the Read Ahead manager's ability to perform as efficiently as possible is somewhat dependent on the organization of the data that it prefetches.

If the data is contiguous in nature, the Read Ahead manager can work very well and read large chunks of data at a time. If the data is scattered and mixed throughout extents that contain other objects, the Read Ahead manager cannot move in one fluid direction and instead must skip around the file(s) to obtain the data it believes will be needed.

As a result, it is desirable to have the object data organized as contiguously as possible. The question is: how can one tell if this is the case? Viewing the extent fragmentation scores for each object is one way, but another way is to view object fragment placements throughout the database. This is best viewed through a third party tool that can visually present the extents in a way that allows one to easily diagnose extent proximity issues, but nonetheless, the *up_bn_storage_map* procedure below is needed to get the raw diagnostic data:

💾 up_bn_storage_map
-- Script is available in the Online Code Depot

Removing Fragmentation

What should be done when fragmentation does indeed exist in one or more of the objects? The standard prescription is to perform a reorganization; however, not all reorganization methods are created equal. There are four main approaches in SQL Server 7 and 2000 that can be taken to perform reorganization. Each approach has its positive and negative points:

- **Drop/Create Index:** This is the most basic way to reorganize indexes; however, this option cannot be used if the index supports a constraint. Plus, it is not the best thing to do during normal business operations, as the index is naturally unavailable for use during construction. Worse yet, for clustered index creations, the entire table is unavailable for use (read or write) and for non-clustered index creations, only read operations are allowed on the parent table.

- **Create Index with *drop_existing:*** This option gets the DBA around the problem of not being able to re-create an index that supports a constraint; however, all other headaches identified above with the drop/create index method still apply.

- **DBCC DBREINDEX:** This method allows the DBA to rebuild one or more indexes without having to know their Data Definition Language (DDL) definition. This command can also be safely issued if the indexes support constraints on a table. Other advantages include the rebuilding of statistics during the operation and the fact that the DBCC command can make use of multi-processor environments and run quite fast in such settings. Drawbacks to this method include the fact that it is also an offline operation and can negate object use during the utility run. It is also an atomic transaction, so if it is stopped before completion, all defragmentation work is lost.

- **DBCC INDEXDEFRAG:** Available for SQL Server 2000 and higher, this method has the distinct advantage of being an online operation, meaning the DBA can reorganize while the objects stay available for use. Unlike DBCC DBREINDEX, this method can be stopped without any of the previous defragmentation work being lost. Of course, there has to be some penalty to pay for all the positives associated with this method. The way DBCC INDEXDEFRAG manages to be an online operation is that it skips over pages that are in use during its run, meaning that it is possible to miss some fragmentation. Also, DBCC INDEXDEFRAG is not as fast as DBCC DBREINDEX because of its inability to use multiple processors for its work, and it doesn't rebuild object statistics. This operation can also make extent scan fragmentation worse. It eliminates extents but does not improve the physical order of the remaining extents.

Tables are not mentioned at all in the above reorganization methods. It is rare to have to rebuild standard heap tables, tables without clustered indexes. Fragmentation matters little in heap tables because the data rows do not have to be kept in order. Further, the SQL Server does a good job of keeping the data pages full because it will reuse space left empty from DELETEs and such. The main space headache facing most heap tables is row forwarding. In the special case in which a heap table is exhibiting signs of fragmentation, a clustered index on the table, with a high *fillfactor*, can be created and the index dropped after completion.

The other option is to copy all the data out of the table, issue a TRUNCATE or drop/recreate the table and copy all the data back in.

In SQL Server 2005, all the previously mentioned options are available, but there are also the two following additions:

- **ALTER INDEX REORGANIZE:** This option reorders the leaf level pages of the index in logical order. The good news is that this operation is online, so concurrency issues will not be encountered. The down side is that it is not as complete as a drop/create statement. This option replaces the DBCC INDEXREFRAG command.

- **ALTER INDEX REBUILD:** This option replaces DBCC DBREINDEX, but is online in nature unless the index is eXtensible Markup Language (XML). It is also possible to rebuild just one or more partitions of an index instead of the entire index.

In SQL Server 2005, the index can also be rebuilt online via the *create index...drop_existing* statement by utilizing the new *online=on* clause. An example of this approach might be:

```
create nonclustered index emp_ssn
    on dbo.emp(emp_ssn)
    with (drop_existing=on,online=on)
go
```

Sometimes, a DBA will reorganize a table or index and no measurable benefits are noticed afterwards. The same or worse fragmentation metrics are observed for the objects in question. What could have gone wrong?

Reorganization Did Not Help!

When attempting the reorganization of either tables or indexes, the DBA must understand that only objects of a significant size will show improvement from reorganization. Microsoft has stated that "objects with less than 1,000 pages" will often offer no performance improvements whatsoever from being reorganized.

Other important points of interest include:

- Tables without indexes receive zero benefit naturally from running either a DBCC DBREINDEX or a DBCC INDEXDEFRAG. The only way to reorganize a table without indexes is to create a clustered index on the table and then immediately drop it or empty the contents of the table into a temporary table, truncate the original table, and then refill it.

- Heap tables should not be diagnosed as having fragmentation through the logical scan fragmentation measure. This metric is meaningless for such tables.

- Small objects seldom benefit from reorganizations. For example, the page density for a table with only 10 rows in it will likely not be high, and reorganizing it will not change things one bit. The DBA needs to keep such things in mind when determining whether to reorganize an object.

- Lack of contiguous free space can result in all fragmentation not being eliminated. Without large amounts of contiguous free space, reorganization operations may have to reuse other areas of space within the database files. Often, the end result is an index being reorganized, but still having an amount of logical scan fragmentation.

Forwarded Rows

SQL Server will move rows in a table under certain conditions. One situation might arise when a row in a table that has a variable-length column is updated to a larger size that will no longer fit on its original page. When SQL Server creates a forwarding pointer, the pointer remains in place unless one of two things happens. The first is when a row shrinks enough to move back to its original location. The second is when the entire database shrinks. When a database file shrinks, SQL Server will reassign the row identifiers, which are used as the row locators, so the shrink process never generates forwarded rows.

At times, forwarded records can reduce performance because additional I/O is involved to first obtain the record pointer to the relocated row, and then the row itself. But, when does row forwarding become a problem? For example, just because a table has one hundred forwarded rows, does that mean a performance problem exists? It depends. If the table has one hundred rows in it, a problem does exist because 100% of the table suffers from forwarded rows. If the table has three million rows, the forwarded row situation involving one hundred rows is likely not causing much fuss in the database.

The fragmentation diagnostic procedures supplied earlier in this chapter will help the DBA identify tables with forwarded row problems. The same holds true for the new SQL Server 2005 *sys.dm_db_index_physical_stats* function. In particular, the procedures provide both a forwarded record count and a forwarded record percent so tables that could benefit from being reorganized can be easily pinpointed.

In terms of removing forwarded rows, the options include reorganizing the table or performing a shrink of a database or database file.

Besides object fragmentation, what other vampire-style bottlenecks might be encountered?

Page Splits

One issue that might crop up is page splitting. When data is added or modified for a table that has indexes, the indexes must be updated as well. As index pages fill up, free space needed to keep index keys in their proper order can often run very low. If an index update needs to be made to a page and no free space exists on that page, SQL Server will perform a page split where it moves approximately half the rows on a page to a new page. Page splits cause additional overhead in the form of CPU usage and I/O. Observing large numbers of page splits can signal a resource bottleneck in the server.

To get a count of page split activity, the following *pagesplit.sql* query can be used:

To avoid page splits, the DBA can look into tuning the *fillfactor* property of an index, which controls the percentage of the index page that is filled during creation. The default value of one hundred tells SQL Server to completely fill each page; whereas, lower numbers tell SQL Server to leave room for additional index rows or updates to existing rows.

Storage Bottleneck Wrap Up

Many thought there was nothing really to worry about with respect to SQL Server storage. As this extensive section has shown, there are indeed things to which the DBA needs to pay strict attention with respect to storage bottlenecks. A constant vigil must be adhered to against both immediate and vampire-style storage bottlenecks so the performance of SQL Server systems is not adversely impacted.

With a thorough presentation of storage bottlenecks out of the way, it is now time to turn attention to diagnosing and correcting bottlenecks within the system area of SQL Server.

System Bottlenecks

Most DBAs have lost count of the number of times someone has called them to complain that the database server seemed slow. Other than statements to the effect that such-and-such activity seems to be taking much longer than normal, specifics are often few. How can one start to troubleshoot a supposedly slow running SQL Server?

The place to start is making the determination of whether the problem is a session-specific issue or a system wide issue. An overall sluggish system will typically result in more than one call to the DBA's desk, plus the DBA can usually log on to check the responsiveness of SQL Server from his own workstation. Most DBAs will keep application-specific SQL queries with which they can test response times on servers that are the target of performance complaints.

Diligent organizations have an application lead, someone that can be trusted, who can perform the same type of tests. It is not uncommon for an application to seem slow, but have the actual underlying SQL queries run just fine. Having an application lead possessing the capability to pull up a Query Analyzer session and test responsiveness in that fashion will sometimes take the burden off of the overloaded DBA's and put it, instead, on some poor networking or application administrator.

However, if the test queries seem to drag and run longer than usual, the server needs troubleshooting. The natural place to start is obtaining diagnostic information that provides information as to what is causing the SQL Server engine to wait. It stands to reason that eliminating such bottlenecks will increase throughput and result in response times that are palatable.

SQL Server's Wait Interface

Wait analysis is well on its way to becoming the new number one way to resolve database server response time issues. Nearly every major database engine, including SQL Server, has introduced a wait event interface that DBAs can use to determine the primary causes of throughput problems. With SQL Server, an undocumented DBCC command is used to get wait data. However before plunging in, there are a few things that need to be done to get the most out of Microsoft's wait interface.

First Figure 5.7 represents the raw output from the DBCC SQLPERF(WAITSTATS) command:

```
dbcc sqlperf(waitstats)
```

	Wait Type	Requests	Wait Time	Signal Wait Time
1	MISCELLANEOUS	0.0	0.0	0.0
2	LCK_M_SCH_S	0.0	0.0	0.0
3	LCK_M_SCH_M	0.0	0.0	0.0
4	LCK_M_S	3.0	861.0	0.0
5	LCK_M_U	0.0	0.0	0.0
6	LCK_M_X	1.0	0.0	0.0
7	LCK_M_IS	0.0	0.0	0.0
8	LCK_M_IU	0.0	0.0	0.0
9	LCK_M_IX	0.0	0.0	0.0
10	LCK_M_SIU	0.0	0.0	0.0
11	LCK_M_SIX	0.0	0.0	0.0
12	LCK_M_UIX	0.0	0.0	0.0
13	LCK_M_BU	0.0	0.0	0.0
14	LCK_M_RS_S	0.0	0.0	0.0
15	LCK_M_RS_U	0.0	0.0	0.0

Figure 5.7: *Example wait diagnostic output.*

In SQL Server 2000, there are nearly eighty different wait types, and in SQL Server 2005, that number grows to somewhere over 120. The first piece of basic information that is received from the DBCC command is a Wait Type, which identifies each kind of wait event. The *wait type* or *name* is fairly cryptic, but with practice, the ability to identify each wait type will be realized.

After the wait type, the DBA will get a count of *requests*, which indicates how many times the wait type has occurred. At first, one might gravitate toward this column as being the most important, but this notion should be resisted and instead the focus place on the next column, which is *wait time*. *wait time* is the most important indicator of how bad a wait event is in terms of actually being a bottleneck.

In terms of an analogy, it can be compared to driving a car and encountering red lights. If a person is driving down a road and approaches a red light, but it turns green before the driver actually decelerates, the red light really did not affect momentum at all. If, however, that person actually has to stop and is delayed at a red light, the trip has become interrupted.

It's not uncommon to notice wait types that have a rather high number of wait requests but have not logged any actual *wait time*. Other wait types will have accumulated quite a bit of *wait time*, and it is these that need to bubble to the top as they are the ones that deserve attention. It is best to break down *wait time* into percentages because it becomes easier to troubleshoot issues when the DBA knows, for example, that network I/O waits are responsible for 90% of all wait time on the SQL Server.

Something else that needs to be done is bogus or idle waits over which SQL Server has no control or that are not actually important in the overall scheme of things should be eliminated. These wait types include:

- *waitfor*
- *sleep*
- *resource_queue*

Including these wait events in diagnostic scripts will skew the percentage numbers, so it is best to eliminate them.

The following *up_bn_waits* procedure is a good one to use to get a handle on the SQL Server wait activity. It allows idle wait events to be included or excluded, calculates wait time percentages, and sorts the output so the DBA can know exactly what system bottlenecks are responsible for the bulk of overall wait time on SQL Server.

⊟ up_bn_waits

```
-- Script is available in the Online Code Depot
```

Figure 5.8 is a partial representation of SQL Server wait statistics.

	wait_type	wait_requests	pct_wait_total	wait_time_secs	pct_wait_time	signal_wait_time	pct_signal_wait_time
4							
5	LCK_M_S	3	.337	6	53.494	30	33.333
6	PAGEIOLATCH_SH	306	34.343	2	20.637	0	.000
7	IO_COMPLETION	128	14.366	2	12.884	60	66.667
8	ASYNC_IO_COMPLETION	4	.449	1	7.073	0	.000
9	PAGEIOLATCH_EX	23	2.581	0	4.045	0	.000
10	WRITELOG	18	2.020	0	1.522	0	.000
11	PAGEIOLATCH_UP	5	.561	0	.345	0	.000
12	MISCELLANEOUS	0	.000	0	.000	0	.000
13	LCK_M_SCH_S	0	.000	0	.000	0	.000
14	LCK_M_SCH_M	0	.000	0	.000	0	.000
15	PAGEIOLATCH_DT	0	.000	0	.000	0	.000
16	TRAN_MARK_NL	0	.000	0	.000	0	.000

Figure 5.8: *Partial output of SQL Server wait statistics.*

OK, So Now What Should be Done?

The *up_bn_waits* stored procedure has been run and output like that shown in Figure 5.8 has been received. It is shown that the *lck_m_s* wait type is responsible for 53% of all the wait time on SQL Server. Great. Now what?

DBAs in the Oracle, SQL Server, Sybase, etc., worlds are instructed to use their database engine's wait interface to troubleshoot issues, but they are never really told what to do after they receive their wait diagnostic data. For example, what exactly is a *lck_m_s* wait type anyway? What can be done to help fix the matter?

A *lck_m_s* wait indicates waits on share locks. This indicates that SQL Server is experiencing transaction management issues, and that locks on the system might be held longer than necessary or that improper isolation levels are being used within transactions. Next, the DBA might run some scripts that give an idea on blocking locks and also reports the amount of overall system lock wait time. Information on this is provided later in this book.

Microsoft has some decent documents that cover each wait type along with providing recommended actions, so one should check out the SQL Server support site as well as the SQL Server Magazine site, which keeps a listing of the same wait facts. For now, the table below that covers some of the most common wait types and offers advice on what to do if they should be encountered can be referenced.

WAIT TYPE	CORRECTIVE ACTIONS
ASYNC_IO_COMPLETION	Asynchronous I/O requests are waiting to complete. Consideration should be given to shifting filegroups/files to lesser utilized drives, checking for proper indexing using Index Tuning Wizard along with full scans and index seeks counters, and examining file I/O, procedures for these given later in book, to see which files are experiencing longest delays via I/O stalls.
CMTHREAD	Indicates waits for memory to be freed up for use. Could indicate a shortage of server RAM or too low of a memory ceiling for SQL Server.
CURSOR	Indicates SQL is waiting to sync up with asynchronous cursors and can point to the excessive use of cursors.
CXPACKET	Waits for parallel processes. Check *max degree of parallelism* configuration parm. Set parm to less than the number of server CPUs but not zero.
EXCHANGE	See CXPACKET.
IO_COMPLETION	This means certain I/O related actions are being delayed. Bulk insert operations, growth of database or log files, high physical I/O SQL, page splitting, and server paging are potential causes. SQL Profiler can be used to ferret out heavy I/O SQL and examine disk and database hot spots with respect to I/O. The I/O Stall column from the *fn_virtualfilestats* function is especially useful in determining which files are experiencing the most delays.
LATCH_	Latches are short term memory locks, with contention possibly arising in the SQL Server caches. Most common on standard tables and ones with text columns. Look into partitioning tables and also look into solving PAGELATCH_UP and LOG waits.
LCK_	Lock waits. Look into blocking lock situations, check overall lock wait time, ensure transactions are being kept short as possible, and make sure that proper isolation levels are being used. Memory shortages may also cause excessive physical I/O and therefore cause locking delays.

WAIT TYPE	CORRECTIVE ACTIONS
LOGMGR	This refers to waits for the Log Writer to start writing a transaction. High waits might warrant transfer transaction logs to faster devices or breaking up long running DML transactions. Check I/O stall amounts from the *fn_virtualfilestats* function.
NETWORKIO	Waits relating to reading/writing to clients on network. Network bandwidth and SQL Server packet sizes are important considerations here. Regarding NIC bandwidth, ensure at least 100mbits is being used. With SQL Server packet sizes, look into switching from the default 4K packet size to something larger if large amounts of data are being sent to/from SQL Server.
OLEDB	This indicates waits for an OLE DB operation to act on its requests. Slow connection speeds or very high transaction rates can cause these. Large bulk inserts, full text operations, linked server calls, and queries that access virtual tables can spawn these waits as well.
PAGEIOLATCH_	Check latch and I/O wait actions.
PAGELATCH_	Used to synchronize access to buffer pages. Indicates cache size insufficiencies and overall memory shortages.
PAGESUPP	Related to CXPACKET.
PIPELINE_	Indicates waits on PIPELINE, which allows multiple operations to be performed such as log cache writes, etc. Check I/O stall amounts from the *fn_virtualfilestats* function and relocate filegroups/files to less utilized devices.
PSS_CHILD	This wait indicates SQL waiting for a child thread within an asynchronous cursor and can point to the excessive use of cursors.
TEMPOBJ	This wait occurs when global temp tables and the like are attempting to be dropped, but are still being used by others.
UMS_THREAD	Waits for worker threads. The number of worker threads can be increased from the default of 255 if need be.
WAITFOR	Caused by WAITFOR delays in T-SQL code.

WAIT TYPE	CORRECTIVE ACTIONS
WRITELOG	Waits for log write requests. Check I/O stall amounts from the *fn_virtualfilestats* function for log files and relocate log filegroups/files to less utilized devices.

Wait Statistics in SQL Server 2005

In SQL Server 2005, the *master.dbo.sysperfinfo* performance table and the new *sys.dm_os_performance_counters* view contain summaries of wait activity. Each object breaks down waits by wait type, like Log buffer waits, includes total wait counts, average wait time, and also includes information on if the wait is in progress.

As of this writing (beta 2 of SQL Server 2005), the counters do not appear to be accurately recording wait activity; however, they will likely be valid once SQL Server 2005 goes General Announcement.

A basic query, *waitsum_2005.sql*, that can be used to get wait information as recorded in the *sys.dm_os_performance_counters* view is:

⊟ waitsum_2005.sql
```
-- Script is available in the Online Code Depot
```

Figure 5.9 is a representation of the output for new wait statistical view in SQL Server 2005.

	wait_type	total_waits	wait_in_progess	avg_wait_time
1	Lock waits	0	No	0
2	Log buffer waits	0	No	0
3	Log write waits	0	No	0
4	Memory grant queue waits	0	No	0
5	Network IO waits	0	No	0
6	Non-Page latch waits	0	No	0
7	Page IO latch waits	0	No	0
8	Page latch waits	0	No	0
9	Thread-safe memory objects waits	0	No	0
10	Transaction ownership waits	0	No	0
11	Wait for the worker	0	No	0
12	Workspace syncronization waits	0	No	0

Figure 5.9: *Example output for new wait statistical view in SQL Server 2005.*

In addition, SQL Server 2005 offers the *sys.dm_os_wait_stats* dynamic management view, which can be substituted for the DBCC SQLPERF(WAITSTATS) command.

Miscellaneous System Bottlenecks

Outside of wait events, a couple of immediate bottlenecks to be aware of are offline and suspect databases. To get a count of both problems for SQL Server 7, the *dbproblem7.sql* script can be used:

🖫 dbproblem7.sql
```
-- Script is available in the Online Code Depot
```

For SQL Server 2000 and above, the *dbproblem8.sql* script can be used:

🖫 dbproblem8.sql
```
-- Script is available in the Online Code Depot
```

Databases are marked suspect by SQL Server if they fail during automatic recovery, which is performed at server startup. If serious damage is experienced by a database during regular uptime, SQL Server will also mark a database as suspect. There should not be any suspect databases on any production server found.

The steps to handling a suspect database will vary from one installation to another; however, the following are some general guidelines that can be used to troubleshoot a suspect database:

- Begin by examining the SQL Server error log for clues as to what caused the database to be marked as suspect.

- It is not unusual for a server to run out of physical disk space on drives used by SQL Server. When this happens, recovery for databases can sometimes fail with the end result being SQL Server marking a database as suspect. To remedy this situation, space should be freed up on the identified drives or files added to the newly marked suspect database. For SQL Server 2000, this can be accomplished by using the stored procedures: *sp_add_data_file_recover_suspect_db* and *sp_add_log_file_recover_suspect_db*. For version 7.0 of SQL Server, the *sp_resetstatus* stored procedure should be used to reset the suspect status flag for the database in question; the ALTER DATABASE command used to add new datafiles to the database, and then the SQL Server stopped/started.

- Many times, suspect databases are caused by SQL Server not being able to access a database or log file. This happens if a particular physical hard drive has become unavailable, but also can occur if another operating system process has obtained exclusive access to a file. If this scenario proves to be true, once the DBA has ensured that the files are available once again to the operating system, the *sp_resetstatus* stored procedure should be used to reset the suspect status flag for the database and then the SQL Server stopped/started.

If none of these solutions are possible for a suspect database, the database will likely have to be restored using the last full and transaction log backups.

Regarding offline databases, it is usually not common to have a database offline on a production server. If a critical database is found offline, it

---

should be placed back online via the *sp_dboption* stored procedure or the ALTER DATABASE command.

Error Log Analysis

Information on system bottlenecks would not be complete without addressing error log analysis. As with every other database engine, SQL Server records informational and system error messages in a rolling, versioned file that can be easily viewed through a number of different avenues such as Enterprise Manager/Management Studio, Windows Event Viewer, etc. There are occasions when SQL Server records messages that alert the DBA to problematic system bottlenecks that require immediate attention, so there needs to be an easy way of identifying them.

When looking at error logs, there are a couple of approaches to take in analyzing activity:

- Have any actual errors occurred?

- What kind of daily volume/activity has the log experienced?

To check if any errors exist in the current SQL Server error log, the following procedure, *up_bn_error_log_count*, which provides a simple count of error messages in the current log can be run.

🖫 up_bn_error_log_count
-- Script is available in the Online Code Depot

Sometimes error counts and analysis of errors is not enough. Perhaps an informational event that affected performance repetitively occurred in the logs for a particular day that was missed. A good way of finding these cyclical, repetitive events is by doing a daily volume analysis over the log to see if any day exploded with messages compared to the others. The following procedure, *up_bn_log_daily_volume*, will break down message volume by day so one can easily see such a thing:

🖫 up_bn_log_daily_volume
-- Script is available in the Online Code Depot

Conclusion

Storage and system bottlenecks have the capacity to easily wreck an otherwise well designed SQL Server, but by using the techniques described in this chapter, it can be ensured the DBA will not be caught off guard by such problems.

The next chapter will explain how to avoid bottlenecks that occur at the session and operating system levels.

Bottleneck Analysis: Part Two

Diagnosing Session and O/S Issues

In reactive environments, most DBAs will discover they have a database bottleneck only when a disgruntled user calls and complains of slow response times. However, even very proactive DBAs will occasionally encounter a solitary session that is experiencing issues that are not representative of the rest of the user base. This being the case, it is wise that a SQL Server DBA be able to quickly troubleshoot individual session issues to uncover bottlenecks that may, sooner or later, come calling on the rest of the community.

If a DBA has worked through the troubleshooting flowchart and has not turned up bottlenecks at the session, system, or storage levels, the problem may very well exist outside of SQL Server, and instead be present at the Windows operating system level. The majority of the time, this is the realm of the system administrator; however, DBAs will, at times, have to confront these issues. Therefore, the DBA should possess competence in diagnosing and documenting basic O/S issues that can affect the performance of SQL Server.

This chapter focuses on the analysis and correction of bottlenecks at the session and operating system level. The first part of this chapter will cover session bottlenecks and will follow up with general advice on how to interrogate the Windows O/S to determine if SQL Server is innocent of any performance wrong-doing.

Session Bottleneck Analysis

When it comes to diagnosing session-based bottlenecks in the SQL Server, the following two broad areas will be focused on:

- Lock Activity
- Waits

Diagnosing Primary Locking Issues

To modify database information or structures, a user session must obtain a lock on the object to perform its task. In addition to user locks, SQL Server itself issues lock requests to carry out its internal duties. A single blocking session has the potential to stop work for nearly all other processes on a small system and can cause major headaches even on large systems.

Blocks are most often caused by user processes holding exclusive locks and not releasing them via a proper COMMIT frequency. Unless a process times out via an application timeout mechanism, or the process has specified a timeout period via the SET LOCK_TIMEOUT command, a process waiting for a lock will wait indefinitely.

In this case, it is critical that the high performance SQL Server DBA be able to quickly understand the locking situation on the database servers and be able to resolve any lock-induced bottlenecks. If a user calls and complains that their databases are hung with no activity taking place, the first thing the DBA should do is see if any blocking locks currently exist on the server. This can easily be accomplished with the *blockcount.sql* query:

💾 blockcount.sql

```
-- ****************************************************
-- Copyright © 2005 by Rampant TechPress
-- This script is free for non-commercial purposes
-- with no warranties.  Use at your own risk.
--
-- To license this script for a commercial purpose,
-- contact info@rampant.cc
```

```
-- **************************************************
select
    count(*)
from
    master.dbo.sysprocesses
where
    blocked <> 0
```

If a non-zero value is returned from the query above, the next step is to obtain detail regarding the blocking lock situation. This involves locating the sessions being blocked as well as the session(s) doing the blocking. The following procedure, *up_bn_locks*, allows the DBA to see either all locks, or by passing a parameter in, restrict the output to only sessions and their lock details that are being blocked.

up_bn_locks
`-- Script is available in the Online Code Depot`

Figure 6.1 is a representation of the sample output from the query on locks on SQL Server.

spid	loginname	ntuser	dbname	tabname	index_id	lock_type	lock_mode	lock_status	lock_ownertype	user_program	blocking_spid
1	51 NT AUTHORITY\SYSTEM	SYSTEM	msdb	[NULL]	0	DATABASE	SHARED	GRANTED	SESSION	SQLAgent - Generic Refresher	0
2	52 NT AUTHORITY\SYSTEM	SYSTEM	msdb	[NULL]	0	DATABASE	SHARED	GRANTED	SESSION	SQLAgent - Alert Engine	0
3	54 sa		er	ADMISSION	2	PAGE	INTENT UPDATE	GRANTED	TRANSACTION	DBArtisan	60
4	54 sa		er	[NULL]	0	DATABASE	SHARED	GRANTED	SESSION	DBArtisan	60
5	54 sa		er	ADMISSION	2	KEY	UPDATE	WAITING	TRANSACTION	DBArtisan	60
6	54 sa		er	ADMISSION	0	TABLE	INTENT EXCLUSIVE	GRANTED	TRANSACTION	DBArtisan	60
7	60 sa		er	ADMISSION	4	KEY	EXCLUSIVE	GRANTED	TRANSACTION	SQL Query Analyzer	0
8	60 sa		er	ADMISSION	2	PAGE	INTENT EXCLUSIVE	GRANTED	TRANSACTION	SQL Query Analyzer	0
9	60 sa		er	ADMISSION	2	KEY	EXCLUSIVE	GRANTED	TRANSACTION	SQL Query Analyzer	0
10	60 sa		er	ADMISSION	0	TABLE	INTENT EXCLUSIVE	GRANTED	TRANSACTION	SQL Query Analyzer	0
11	60 sa		er	ADMISSION	0	PAGE	INTENT EXCLUSIVE	GRANTED	TRANSACTION	SQL Query Analyzer	0
12	60 sa		er	[NULL]	0	DATABASE	SHARED	GRANTED	SESSION	SQL Query Analyzer	0
13	60 sa		er	ADMISSION	0	PAGE	INTENT EXCLUSIVE	GRANTED	TRANSACTION	SQL Query Analyzer	0
14	60 sa		er	ADMISSION	0	RID	EXCLUSIVE	GRANTED	TRANSACTION	SQL Query Analyzer	0
15	60 sa		er	ADMISSION	0	PAGE	INTENT EXCLUSIVE	GRANTED	TRANSACTION	SQL Query Analyzer	0
16	60 sa		er	ADMISSION	3	KEY	EXCLUSIVE	GRANTED	TRANSACTION	SQL Query Analyzer	0

Figure 6.1: *Sample output showing detail for all locks on SQL Server.*

For SQL Server 2005, the *master.dbo.syslockinfo* table in the previous procedure can be replaced with the *sys.dm_tran_locks* dyanmic management view.

If the DBA needs to know what SQL is being issued for the SPID's either being blocked or blocking other sessions, a DBCC INPUTBUFFER () command can be issued and the SPID's of interest can be passed in. If a decent cursory or analytic type monitor is being used, all of this information can easily be brought up without the use of scripts or commands as shown in Figure 6.2 below:

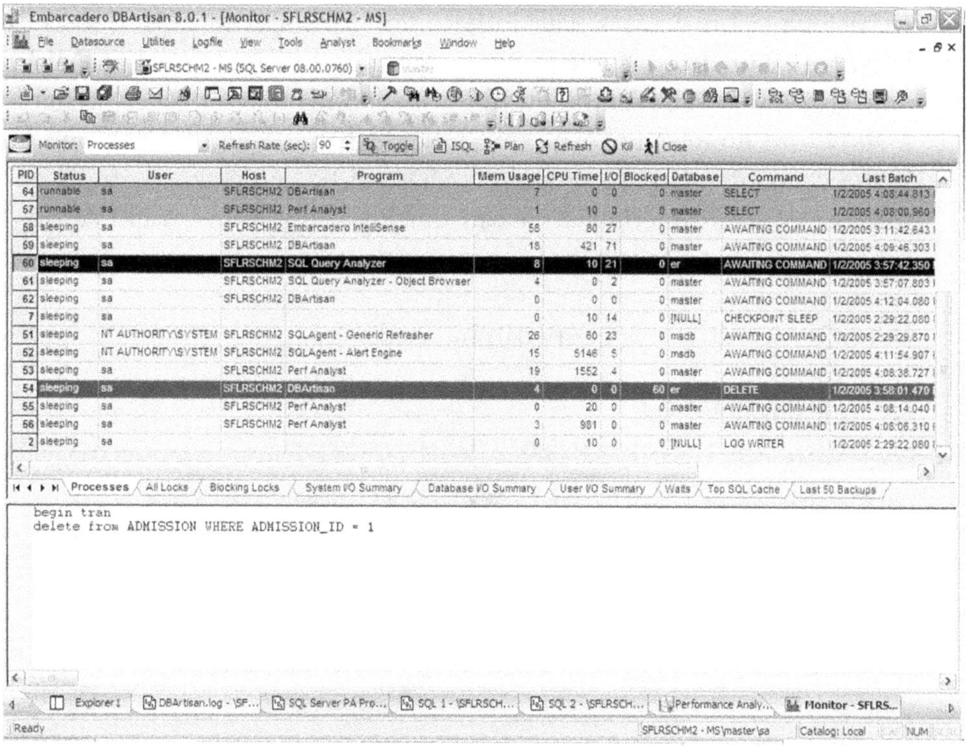

Figure 6.2: *SQL Server monitor showing blocking lock info along with SQL.*

Once discovered, a blocking lock situation can normally be quickly remedied. The DBA simply has to issue a KILL against the offending process, which eliminates the stranglehold on the objects the user was accessing. Other user processes will then almost always complete in an instant. However, unlike fixing a current blocking lock problem, preventing the blocking lock situation in the first place is tricky.

The culprit of blocking lock scenarios is usually the application design or the SQL being used within the application itself. Properly coding an application to reference database objects in an efficient order and using the right SQL to get the job done is an art. The key to avoiding lock contention is to process user transactions in the quickest and most efficient manner possible. This is not always easy to do.

By default, all processes wait indefinitely for locks in SQL Server. This behavior can be changed by using the SET LOCK_TIMEOUT command, which limits the number of seconds that a process waits for a lock before timing out. The question might be asked, "How one know if the timeout was set too short?" The SQL Server keeps track of the number of lock timeouts so it can quickly show if an invalid setting for timeouts has been received.

For SQL Server 7, this query can be used:

🖫 lock_timeouts7.sql

```
-- ************************************************
-- Copyright © 2005 by Rampant TechPress
-- This script is free for non-commercial purposes
-- with no warranties.  Use at your own risk.
--
-- To license this script for a commercial purpose,
-- contact info@rampant.cc
-- ************************************************

select
    sum(cntr_value)
from
    master.dbo.sysperfinfo
where
    counter_name = 'Lock Timeouts/sec' and
    object_name = 'SQLServer:Locks'
```

For SQL Server 2000 and above, the following query can be used:

🖫 lock_timeouts8.sql

```
-- ************************************************
-- Copyright © 2005 by Rampant TechPress
-- This script is free for non-commercial purposes
-- with no warranties.  Use at your own risk.
--
-- To license this script for a commercial purpose,
-- contact info@rampant.cc
-- ************************************************

select
    cntr_value
from
```

```
    master.dbo.sysperfinfo
where
    counter_name = 'Lock Timeouts/sec' and
    object_name = 'SQLServer:Locks' and
    instance_name = '_Total'
```

Additional Lock Analysis

There are other forms of lock analysis that can be performed if the DBA desires to investigate how badly lock contention is affecting SQL Server. The primary metric to review is the amount of lock wait time associated with issued SQL. Blocking locks will cause users pain only if they are prolonged in nature. That's why the best performance monitors only notify the DBA of a blocking lock problem when its block time exceeds a customized block duration threshold.

SQL Server offers a number of other lock counters via the *master.dbo.sysperfinfo* table that can be used to check lock activity. The following queries for SQL Server 7 and for SQL Server 2000 and above can get this information in short order:

⊟ lock_analysis7.sql

```
-- **************************************************
-- Copyright © 2005 by Rampant TechPress
-- This script is free for non-commercial purposes
-- with no warranties.  Use at your own risk.
--
-- To license this script for a commercial purpose,
-- contact info@rampant.cc
-- **************************************************

select
    counter_name,
    sum(cntr_value)
from
    master.dbo.sysperfinfo
where
    counter_name in ('Lock Wait Time (ms)',
                     'Average Wait Time (ms)',
                     'Lock Waits/sec') and
    object_name = 'SQLServer:Locks'
group by
    counter_name
```

⊟ lock_analysis8.sql

```
-- **************************************************
-- Copyright © 2005 by Rampant TechPress
```

```
-- This script is free for non-commercial purposes
-- with no warranties.  Use at your own risk.
--
-- To license this script for a commercial purpose,
-- contact info@rampant.cc
-- *************************************************

select
    counter_name,
    sum(cntr_value)
from
    master.dbo.sysperfinfo
where
    counter_name in ('Lock Wait Time (ms)',
                     'Average Wait Time (ms)',
                     'Lock Waits/sec') and
    instance_name = '_Total' and
    object_name = 'SQLServer:Locks'
group by
    counter_name
```

The output from these queries will reveal the overall wait time in milliseconds so the DBA will have a decent understanding of the number of lock waits and about how long each took.

Deadlocks

Deadlocks or deadly embraces as they are called on other database platforms occur when processes cannot proceed because they are waiting on a set of resources held by each other or held by other processes. Deadlock problems are a serious red flag that application design issues exist in the database.

It is easy to understand whether or not there is a deadlock problem. Depending on the SQL Server version, one of the two following queries can be used to get a count of deadlocks, the first being for SQL Server 7, and the other being for 2000 and higher:

📁 **deadlock7.sql**

```
-- *************************************************
-- Copyright © 2005 by Rampant TechPress
-- This script is free for non-commercial purposes
-- with no warranties.  Use at your own risk.
--
-- To license this script for a commercial purpose,
-- contact info@rampant.cc
-- *************************************************
```

```
select
    sum(cntr_value)
from
    master.dbo.sysperfinfo
where
    object_name = 'SQLServer:Locks' and
    counter_name = 'Number of Deadlocks/sec'
```

🖫 deadlock8.sql

```
-- ************************************************
-- Copyright © 2005 by Rampant TechPress
-- This script is free for non-commercial purposes
-- with no warranties.  Use at your own risk.
--
-- To license this script for a commercial purpose,
-- contact info@rampant.cc
-- ************************************************

select
    cntr_value
from
    master.dbo.sysperfinfo
where
    object_name = 'SQLServer:Locks' and
    counter_name = 'Number of Deadlocks/sec' and
    instance_name = '_Total'
```

Consistently seeing deadlock counts greater than zero will indicate that some user processes are experiencing delays in completing their work.

When SQL Server identifies a deadlock, it resolves the situation by choosing the process that can break the deadlock. This process is called the deadlock victim. SQL Server rolls back the deadlock victim's transaction, and notifies the process application by returning an error message. It also cancels the process' request and allows the transactions of the remaining processes to continue. SQL Server always attempts to choose the least expensive thread running the transaction as the deadlock victim.

Because SQL Server automatically resolves deadlock situations, proactive work should be performed to prevent them in the first place. As has already been stated, the culprit of most blocking lock and deadlock scenarios is usually the application design or the SQL being used within the application itself.

The default deadlock behavior can be changed by using the SET DEADLOCK_PRIORITY command, which reprioritizes a process' position in a deadlock situation. The source of deadlocks can also be identified through some tracing commands.

By enabling the trace flags 3605 and 1204 via the *DBCC* TRACEON command, SQL Server can be instructed to write detailed deadlock activity to its error log. In the error log, the types of SQL statements involved in a deadlock can be seen. Also, the *rowid* of the row and object page involved in the deadlock will be received. Armed with this information, the DBCC PAGE command can be used to actually find the object that caused the deadlock.

Examining Session Waits

Unfortunately, the SQL Server does not have as robust a session wait interface as Oracle does; however, there are a few diagnostic metrics that can be utilized to get a feel for session wait activity. The *master.dbo.sysprocesses* table contains a row for every session connected to SQL Server. If a session is waiting for any reason, SQL Server will record the wait type and wait time in two of the columns in *master.dbo.sysprocesses*. While this helps diagnose an in-process wait, the drawback to this implementation is that when another wait for the session occurs, the wait information is overwritten, so in reality, there is no history from which to work.

The *sesswait.sql* query below will help the DBA get a handle on current session wait activity and will bubble to the top the processes with the highest percentage of overall wait time.

🖫 sesswait.sql
-- Script is available in the Online Code Depot

Figure 6.3 shows a representation of the output of the above query.

	spid	loginame	windows_user	database_name	status	program_name	lastwaittype	wait_time_secs	pct_total_wait_time
1	14	sa		master	suspended		DBMIRROR_EVENTS_QUEUE	460936.3	98.35
2	9	sa		master	suspended		CHECKPOINT_QUEUE	7675.517	1.63
3	3	sa		master	suspended		LOGMGR_QUEUE	37.674	.00
4	10	sa		master	sleeping		MISCELLANEOUS	0	.00
5	11	sa		master	sleeping		MISCELLANEOUS	0	.00
6	16	sa		master	sleeping		MISCELLANEOUS	0	.00
7	17	sa		master	sleeping		MISCELLANEOUS	0	.00
8	18	sa		master	sleeping		MISCELLANEOUS	0	.00
9	19	sa		master	sleeping		MISCELLANEOUS	0	.00
10	21	sa		master	sleeping		MISCELLANEOUS	0	.00
11	22	sa		master	sleeping		MISCELLANEOUS	0	.00
12	23	sa		master	sleeping		MISCELLANEOUS	0	.00
13	24	sa		master	sleeping		MISCELLANEOUS	0	.00
14	25	sa		master	sleeping		MISCELLANEOUS	0	.00
15	51	NT AUTHORITY\SYSTEM	SYSTEM	ReportServer	sleeping	.Net SqlClient Data Provider	MISCELLANEOUS	0	.00
16	52	NT AUTHORITY\SYSTEM	SYSTEM	msdb	sleeping	SQLAgent - Subsystems refresher	MISCELLANEOUS	0	.00
17	53	NT AUTHORITY\SYSTEM	SYSTEM	ReportServer	sleeping	.Net SqlClient Data Provider	MISCELLANEOUS	0	.00
18	54	NT AUTHORITY\SYSTEM	SYSTEM	ReportServer	sleeping	.Net SqlClient Data Provider	MISCELLANEOUS	0	.00
19	55	sa		master	sleeping	DBArtisan	MISCELLANEOUS	0	.00
20	56	NT AUTHORITY\SYSTEM	SYSTEM	msdb	sleeping	SQLAgent - Generic Refresher	MISCELLANEOUS	0	.00
21	57	NT AUTHORITY\SYSTEM	SYSTEM	msdb	sleeping	SQLAgent - Alert Engine	MISCELLANEOUS	0	.00

Figure 6.3: *Sample output showing session wait activity.*

In SQL Server 2005, the *sys.dm_os_waiting_tasks* dynamic management view can be utilized to get much of the same data as that shown in Figure 6.3; although as of this writing, it does not offer a set of information that is as complete.

Operating System Bottleneck Analysis

The topic of tuning a Windows server is beyond the scope of this book. While such work is normally assigned to Windows system administrators, a SQL Server DBA should be able to interrogate a server box to determine if there are obvious issues at the Windows layer that are affecting the overall performance of the Microsoft database. The following section will explain a few methods that a SQL Server DBA can use to see if Windows is putting a stranglehold on their SQL Server.

Windows Bottleneck Checklist

When looking into potential bottlenecks at the Windows O/S level, the DBA will make heavy use of Microsoft's supplied performance counters. Such counters can be accessed through the Windows Performance monitor and other standard Windows monitors.

The following table, Table 6.1, can be used when investigating possible Windows server-related bottlenecks. It contains the counter name, description and possible courses of action.

COUNTER NAME	DESCRIPTION/ACTION
Memory: Available Bytes	Reflects the amount of free RAM on the server. If there is little to no free memory left, SQL Server's memory usage should be checked to see if total memory is near or at the target memory counters. If true, insufficient server memory is indicated for SQL Server. If false, perhaps the server has too many other memory hungry applications running on it.
Memory: Pages/sec	Indicates paging activity on Windows. On SQL Server dedicated machines, the counter should remain close to zero. Higher values signal memory pressure.
Physical Disk: Avg. Disk Queue Length	Indicates average of disk queues. Values of two times the number of disk drives or higher for prolonged period signal I/O bottlenecks on associated disk arrays. Heavy SQL Server waits should be identified to see if SQL Server is being impacted.
Physical Disk: Current Queue Length	See Avg. Disk Queue Length.
Processor: % Processor Time	Reflects percentage of time that the CPU is executing work. Spikes are common, but sustained percentage readings of 80-90% over long periods of time may indicate a CPU or CPU cache insufficiency.
Processor: %User Time	Amount of user process time. Should not exceed 70-80% on servers dedicated to SQL Server
System: Processor Queue Length	The CPU queue. Higher values (2 or more) over prolonged periods indicate a CPU bottleneck.

Table 6.1: *Performance counters and their definitions*

Correlating Windows Metrics with SQL Server Statistics

Another reason it is good for SQL Server DBAs to have a working knowledge of Windows O/S metrics is so they can help confirm a performance diagnosis that is being made at the database level. For example, seeing IO_COMPLETION waits via the SQL Server DBCC SQLPERF(WAITSTATS) command would indicate a possible I/O completion bottleneck in the database, which can be confirmed by examining the Avg. Disk Queue Length Windows performance counter.

Table 6.2 below correlates some of the wait events introduced in the previous chapter with Windows performance counters. This will give the DBA more ammunition with which to make a sound call on a bottleneck that has been identified.

IF THESE WAITS APPEAR IN SQL SERVER...	... CHECK THESE ON THE SERVER
ASYNC_IO_COMPLETION	Physical Disk: Avg. Disk Queue Length Physical Disk: Current Queue Length Memory: Available Bytes Memory: Pages/sec
IO_COMPLETION	Physical Disk: Avg. Disk Queue Length Physical Disk: Current Queue Length Memory: Available Bytes Memory: Pages/sec
LATCH_	Memory: Available Bytes Memory: Pages/sec
LOGMGR	Physical Disk: Avg. Disk Queue Length Physical Disk: Current Queue Length
OLEDB	Physical Disk: Avg. Disk Queue Length Physical Disk: Current Queue Length
PAGEIOLATCH_	Physical Disk: Avg. Disk Queue Length Physical Disk: Current Queue Length
PAGELATCH_	Physical Disk: Avg. Disk Queue Length Physical Disk: Current Queue Length
PAGESUPP	Physical Disk: Avg. Disk Queue Length Physical Disk: Current Queue Length
WRITELOG	Physical Disk: Avg. Disk Queue Length Physical Disk: Current Queue Length

Table 6.2: *Wait events correlated with Windows performance counters*

Conclusion

The areas broadly examined by the bottleneck analysis methodology are rounded out with the interrogation of sessions and the Windows operating system. Being able to pinpoint issues with a singular session or at the server level will help the DBA cover all the bases when it comes to applying this primary analysis method. The next chapter will look at the next most important performance methodology: workload analysis.

Workload Analysis

Unlocking the Who, What, and Why of Performance Problems

Although bottleneck analysis should be the primary analytic method for troubleshooting SQL Server performance, workload analysis will be right on its heels as the next technique that should be implemented. With workload analysis, the DBA begins the process of unlocking the who, what, and why of performance issues and uncovering where the majority of SQL Server resources are being used.

When using workload analysis, the DBA will typically work through four layers of SQL Server. Those layers are:

- Global Server Workload
- Database Workload
- Session Workload
- SQL Workload

This chapter will examine each layer in detail and provide ways to diagnose and correct excessive resource workload/usage in SQL Server.

Server Workload Analysis

In truth, server workload analysis is not the best judge of overall SQL Server health. This is primarily due to the fact most of the available statistics are cumulative in nature and are not much use for a server that has been up a long time. Some third party monitors and the Windows NT performance monitor get around this problem by calculating delta

---

measures between the monitor's sampling intervals. This makes it much easier to see spikes in, for example, physical I/O.

However, the DBA can still get a feel for overworked servers by running a few SQL scripts and stored procedures. In general, the following three areas will be reviewed in this book:

- I/O
- CPU
- Memory

This chapter will focus on I/O and CPU usage, while the following chapter will explain memory workload.

One somewhat antiquated method of obtaining base CPU and I/O metrics is to run the *sp_monitor* stored procedure. This procedure provides core measurements as to the magnitude of CPU activity, read and write activity and etc. The procedure gives the DBA an idea about changes between the measurements from the time the last iteration of *sp_monitor* was run until the current run. Although this is helpful, it is very dependent on the DBA continually issuing the command to obtain the data.

Examining CPU Activity

In terms of CPU activity, a query can be issued and the system statistical function @@CPU_BUSY can be selected. It shows time in milliseconds

that the CPU has spent working since SQL Server was started. This is a steadily increasing number and is best viewed via a monitor or procedure that can compute differences between sampled intervals, along with a comparison of @@IDLE. This function is a millisecond measurement of how idle SQL Server has been since startup.

Some sources indicate that @@CPU_BUSY has to be multiplied by @@TIMETICKS to get the actual time in milliseconds. This claim does not appear to be valid. Testing by some savvy SQL Server DBAs has determined that @@CPU_BUSY has to be multiplied by @@TIMETICKS and then divided by the number of CPUs on the server to get the actual time. To validate this on the box, the following *test_time* T-SQL code can be run:

🖫 test_time.sql
```
-- Script is available in the Online Code Depot
```

The CPU count number of four in the above T-SQL code would have to be replaced with the actual number of processors the machine has in order to get the proper numbers out on the box.

The easiest approach to obtaining current CPU activity is to simply use the Microsoft Task Manager and locate SQL Server executable. Task Manager can give real time and historical peaks/dips that have occurred since the monitor has been running. Figure 7.1 is a representation of the Windows Task Manager process monitor.

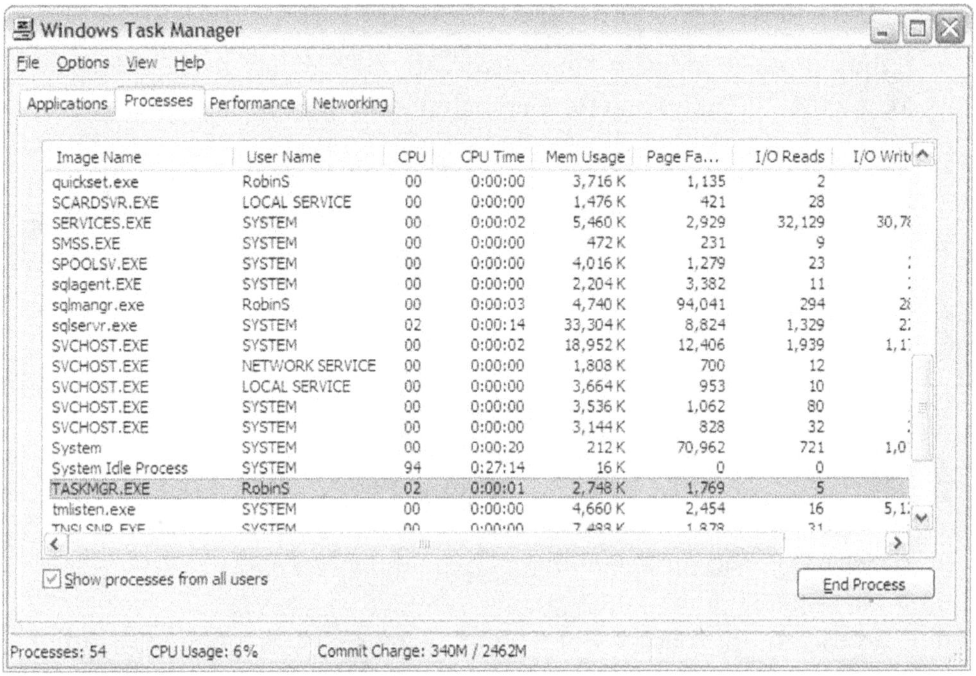

Figure 7.1: *Microsoft Task Manager Monitor.*

Server I/O

When examining overall server I/O, there are two categories that the DBA will review. The first is basic physical I/O, which covers reads, writes, and etc. The second is more database activity centric and focuses on how objects are being accessed in addition to other general database-related activities. All of these statistics can be accessed via the Windows Performance Monitor or through the *master.dbo.sysperfinfo* table.

Starting with standard physical I/O, the metrics that should be reviewed revolve around SQL Server's pace of moving data from disk to memory as well as its work in managing space. The following query helps the DBA get a handle on these things:

🖫 **server_IO.sql**

-- Script is available in the Online Code Depot

The data received is cumulative and can be difficult to use in a meaningful way. However, there are a few red flags that can be spotted from the results of the above query. On the base physical I/O side, seeing increasing volumes of Readahead Pages can indicate scan activity, as SQL Server will try to pre-read data it thinks it will need to satisfy significant query requests. Large readings for extents allocated can signify that data volumes are substantially increasing through standard insert activity or BCP operations. Heavy freespace scans, which represent the number of scans performed by SQL Server to locate free space for an incoming record, can confirm this as well.

Perhaps the most worrisome statistic is a sharply increasing page splits measure. When data is inserted or updated in a table, SQL Server might reorganize the storage of the data in the table's index pages. When an index page becomes full but a DML operation demands room on that page, SQL Server moves about half the rows to a new page to accommodate the request.

This reorganization is known as a page split. Performance for DML actions can be impaired by page split operations as page splits cause additional overhead in the form of CPU usage and I/O. In addition, more index pages can make for longer index scan times.

To avoid page splits, the *fillfactor* property of an index, which controls the percentage of the index page filled during creation, should be tuned. The default value of zero tells SQL Server to completely fill each page. Actually, SQL Server will leave a little room in the upper level, whereas lower numbers tell SQL Server to leave room for additional index rows or updates to existing rows.

The next set of statistics to examine concern how busy SQL Server is with general database activity. The following *db_activity.sql* query can be used for SQL Server 2000 and higher:

⊟ db_activity.sql
```
-- Script is available in the Online Code Depot
```

These cumulative-wide metrics can be broken down by database, so the DBA can see which databases are experiencing the most action.

Another good query that shows query object access patterns is the *server_object_access.sql* script. This query helps the DBA understand scan and index activity:

🖫 server_object_access.sql
-- Script is available in the Online Code Depot

The output from this query is helpful on a number of different fronts with most every metric giving insight into how SQL Server is accessing database objects. Forwarded records represent the number of records fetched through forwarded record pointers. At times, forwarded records can reduce performance because additional I/O is involved to first obtain the record pointer to the relocated row, and then the row itself is read.

When SQL Server creates a forwarding pointer, it remains in place unless one of two things happens. The first is when a row shrinks enough to move back to its original location. The second is when the entire database shrinks. When a database file shrinks, SQL Server reassigns the row identifiers used as row locators, so the shrink process never generates forwarded rows.

If consistent numbers are present for forward record fetches, the databases should be examined to see which tables have forwarded records. This can be accomplished easily with the procedures given in Chapter 5 of this book. These procedures express the amount of forwarded records in a table as a percentage of overall rows.

Another way to see the total count of forwarded records in a table is to enable trace flag 2509 and execute the DBCC CHECKTABLE command. The output should display the number of forwarded records

---

in that table. Tables with many forwarded records could be candidates for table reorganization.

With respect to the full scans metric, full scans of moderately sized indexes or tables are generally okay. SQL Server can scan and cache a small table much faster than using its index to navigate to any requested data. Full, unrestricted, large table scans, however, are typically not good and degrade overall system performance and response time.

Full scans occur if a table is inadequately indexed or if SQL Server truly needs to access all rows in a table or index to satisfy a query. Calls to UPDATE STATISTICS can also cause full scans.

Unnecessary scans on large tables are something to avoid. If present, they can be a signal for the DBA to investigate the use of more indexes and to review SQL access through EXPLAIN plans. As already mentioned, small table scans are actually a good thing because SQL Server can often cache the entire table in a single I/O operation.

Large numbers of index searches and probe scans are typically desirable as well, because they can lead to the fastest possible resolution to data access requests. The index search metric represents the total number of index searches. Index searches are normally used to start range scans for single index record fetches and can be used to reposition an index. Probe scans are used in SQL Server to directly find rows in an index or base table.

Once an idea of workload at the global server level has been received, the DBA is ready to drill down and examine workload at the database level to locate the ones leading the charge in terms of resource usage.

Database Workload Analysis

SQL Server, unlike Oracle, is a shared environment in which many databases compete for memory and background process (lazy writer, etc.) attention. This being the case, it is smart to identify if any databases are using the lion's share of resources. Pinpointing these workload hogs can help direct the DBA to the root cause of any sluggishness exhibited by SQL Server.

For databases, the process begins by a review of overall resource consumption and activity. In this process, the DBA is looking for any databases that seem to stand out from the others in terms of overall usage and dynamics. On the resource usage front, a good query to use for this process is the *dbusage_overview.sql* query:

🖫 dbusage_overview.sql
-- Script is available in the Online Code Depot

Figure 7.2 is a representation of the results of the query.

	DB	DBCC Logical Scans	Transactions/sec	Active Transactions	Bulk Copy Rows	Bulk Copy Throughput	Log Cache Reads	Log Flushes	Log Growths	Log Shrinks
1	Anadb	7880704	4499	0	0	0	0	50	0	0
2	big_database	5963776	4489	0	0	0	0	2	0	0
3	CADB	8929280	6522	0	0	0	0	2015	11	0
4	comprepo	5324800	4486	0	0	0	0	2	0	0
5	dtrep	7028736	4486	0	0	0	0	2	0	0
6	er	128786432	4513	0	0	0	0	50	0	0
7	Extreme	1727119360	122076	0	0	0	0	2	0	0
8	gim	5750784	4486	0	0	0	0	2	0	0
9	gpt	24002560	4565	0	0	0	0	2	0	0
10	lumigent	798687232	52843	0	0	0	0	38764	0	2
11	master	78422016	5487	0	0	0	0	90	0	0
12	model	4472832	4119	0	0	0	0	4	0	0
13	msdb	29163520	58130	0	0	0	0	312	0	0
14	Northwind	5537792	4119	0	0	0	0	2	0	0
15	perf_db	11649024	4562	0	0	0	0	2	0	0
16	Petstore	5111808	4484	0	0	0	0	2	0	0
17	pman_db	347693056	52744	0	0	0	84958	48152	0	0
18	pubs	5537792	4119	0	0	0	0	2	0	0
19	tempdb	42737664	852214	0	0	0	0	12437	4	0

Figure 7.2: *Sample output showing overview of database resource usage.*

The query does a nice job of showing which databases are currently responsible for the most resource usage. For example, Figure 7.2 shows that the MASTER database has experienced the most wait time, while the MSDB database has used the most CPU.

After performing the above query, the DBA can then try to get a handle on the types of activities that have gone on in each database by issuing the *dbactivity_overview* query:

🖫 dbactivity_overview

```
-- Script is available in the Online Code Depot
```

Figure 7.3 is a representation of the results of the above query showing an overview of database activity.

	DB	DBCC Logical Scans	Transactions/sec	Active Transactions	Bulk Copy Rows	Bulk Copy Throughput	Log Cache Reads	Log Flushes	Log Growths	Log Shrinks
1	Anadb	0	417	0	0	0	0	22	0	0
2	big_database	0	415	0	0	0	0	2	0	0
3	CADB	0	808	0	0	0	0	363	0	0
4	comprepo	0	412	0	0	0	0	2	0	0
5	dtrep	0	412	0	0	0	0	2	0	0
6	er	0	423	0	0	0	0	24	0	0
7	Extreme	665116672	48449	0	0	0	0	2	0	0
8	gim	0	412	0	0	0	0	2	0	0
9	gpt	0	413	0	0	0	0	2	0	0
10	lumigent	0	414	0	0	0	0	2	0	0
11	master	0	584	0	0	0	0	24	0	0
12	model	0	412	0	0	0	0	4	0	0
13	msdb	0	22393	0	0	0	0	144	0	0
14	Northwind	0	412	0	0	0	0	2	0	0
15	perf_db	0	412	0	0	0	0	2	0	0
16	Petstore	0	412	0	0	0	0	2	0	0
17	pman_db	0	20399	0	0	0	35216	19934	0	0
18	pubs	0	412	0	0	0	0	2	0	0
19	tempdb	0	264525	0	0	0	0	2645	1	0

Figure 7.3: *Overview of database activity.*

This query helps the DBA understand which databases are seeing transaction log extends, and which ones are experiencing the most transactions, etc. Once armed with usage and activity information, applications and databases responsible for the primary workload on SQL Server become more apparent.

Getting Database I/O Details

If I/O activity appears to be high, more information regarding I/O specifics for SQL Server 2000 and higher can be obtained. For SQL Server 2000 and 2005, I/O details for databases and files can be obtained, and for SQL Server 2005, the DBA can drill down a little further and get I/O at the object level.

To get I/O statistics for files and databases in SQL Server 2000, the following two procedures, which presents I/O metrics for all files and databases on a SQL Server can be used:

🖫 **up_wl_file_io**

```
This script is combined with the following script
```

```
-- Script is available in the Online Code Depot
```

💾 up_wl_file_stats

```
-- Script is available in the Online Code Depot
```

Executing the *up_wl_file_io* procedure will provide statistics such as those represented in Figure 7.4 below:

	dbname	fileid	logical_name	dbfilename	reads	writes	bytes_read	bytes_written	iostall
1	Anadb	1	Anadb_Data	C:\Program Files\Microsoft SQL Server\MSSQL\data\Anadb_data.mdf	39.00	2.00	663552.00	16384.00	932
2	Anadb	2	Anadb_Log	C:\Program Files\Microsoft SQL Server\MSSQL\data\Anadb_log.ldf	9.00	6.00	274432.00	109568.00	741
3	big_database	1	big_database_Data	C:\Program Files\Microsoft SQL Server\MSSQL\data\big_database_Data.MDF	71.00	2.00	2990080.00	16384.00	4256
4	big_database	2	big_database_Log	C:\Program Files\Microsoft SQL Server\MSSQL\data\big_database_Log.LDF	9.00	6.00	274432.00	140288.00	370
5	CADB	1	CADB	C:\Program Files\Microsoft SQL Server\MSSQL\data\CADB.mdf	109.00	3.00	1376256.00	24576.00	921
6	CADB	2	CADB_log	C:\Program Files\Microsoft SQL Server\MSSQL\data\CADB_log.LDF	28.00	436.00	356352.00	655872.00	400
7	comprepo	1	quest_ix_repository_Data	C:\Program Files\Microsoft SQL Server\MSSQL\data\quest_ix_repository_data.mdf	30.00	2.00	647168.00	16384.00	460
8	comprepo	2	quest_ix_repository_Log	C:\Program Files\Microsoft SQL Server\MSSQL\data\quest_ix_repository_log.ldf	9.00	5.00	117248.00	26112.00	300
9	dtrep	1	dtrep	C:\Program Files\Microsoft SQL Server\MSSQL\data\dtrep.mdf	35.00	2.00	688128.00	16384.00	400
10	dtrep	2	dtrep_log	C:\Program Files\Microsoft SQL Server\MSSQL\data\dtrep_log.LDF	16.00	5.00	198144.00	43520.00	180
11	er	1	erdata	C:\Program Files\Microsoft SQL Server\MSSQL\erdata.mdf	37.00	2.00	704512.00	16384.00	391
12	er	2	erlog	C:\Program Files\Microsoft SQL Server\MSSQL\erlog.ldf	9.00	6.00	274432.00	140288.00	371
13	Extreme	1	Extreme	C:\Program Files\Microsoft SQL Server\MSSQL\data\Extreme.mdf	897.00	5.00	7798784.00	16384.00	1815
14	Extreme	2	Extreme_log	C:\Program Files\Microsoft SQL Server\MSSQL\data\Extreme_log.LDF	7.00	5.00	195072.00	54784.00	121
15	gim	1	gimdata	C:\Program Files\Microsoft SQL Server\MSSQL\gimdata.mdf	30.00	2.00	647168.00	16384.00	791
16	gim	2	gimlog	C:\Program Files\Microsoft SQL Server\MSSQL\gimlog.ldf	9.00	6.00	274432.00	140288.00	430
17	gpt	1	GPSNew_Data	C:\Program Files\Microsoft SQL Server\MSSQL\data\gpt_Data.MDF	63.00	2.00	1540096.00	16384.00	1622
18	gpt	2	GPSNew_Log	C:\Program Files\Microsoft SQL Server\MSSQL\data\gpt_Log.LDF	9.00	6.00	274432.00	140288.00	1121
19	lumigent	1	lumigent	C:\Program Files\Microsoft SQL Server\MSSQL\data\lumigent.mdf	57.00	2.00	2359296.00	16384.00	5477
20	lumigent	2	lumigent_log	C:\Program Files\Microsoft SQL Server\MSSQL\data\lumigent_log.LDF	7.00	6.00	266240.00	140288.00	250

Figure 7.4: *Example output of database and file I/O metrics.*

From an activity interest standpoint, the DBA should certainly want to pay attention to the reads and writes columns as those columns will reveal which database is under the most I/O duress. From a throughput viewpoint, the *iostall* column should be zeroed in on as it will reveal which files are experiencing the most delays in terms of accomplishing I/O goals. The higher the *iostall*, the worse the files are doing. These files are likely candidates for physical disk relocation or other such actions.

With SQL Server 2005, more detail on the *iostall* issue can be obtained. The *iostall* column returned from the *fn_virtualfilestats* function is broken out into two columns: *IoStallReadMS* and *IoStallWriteMS*. These columns give details, in milliseconds, regarding read and write throughput problems for each file. With this new granular information, it can be determined if read or write problems are causing the issues instead of just I/O in general.

This SQL Server 2005 enhancement means the procedures above need to be altered to account for the *iostall* column being broken up into two columns. The temporary table holding the I/O statistical data must be changed, as does the INSERT statement that inserts file metric info into it and the final SELECT, which presents the information.

SQL Server 2005 presents an easy way to drill deeper in order to retrieve actual object I/O statistical data. The *sys.dm_db_index_operational_stats* function provides good data that helps pinpoint hot objects in various databases. This function can be used to get data back on: an entire SQL Server but is not recommended if there are many of databases and objects; a particular database; or a specific object. There are many columns returned by the function, but the *object_io.sql* query below will give some of the most interesting statistics that will help reveal the objects under heavy I/O pressure:

🖫 object_io.sql

```
-- Script is available in the Online Code Depot
```

The above query uses the current database as an example, but a database name can be fed to the query if the DBA desires to run it outside of the database for which statistics are desired. Again, this query will help uncover hub objects in key databases that may benefit from better indexing, partitioning, reorganization, or relocation to lesser-used physical devices so response times may be reduced. Special attention must be paid to the *range_scans, forwarded_fetches*, and *wait time* columns.

Reducing Backup and Recovery Impact

SQL Server has always offered online backup capabilities with SQL Server 2005 now offering online restoration. This capability is great because users do not have to be evicted from a database to do a backup. However, backup operations definitely come with an overhead price, so it is important that backups are scheduled during off hours, if possible, to minimize the performance hit of completing a backup. If one assumes that performing backups during off hours is not always an option, is there anything that can be done to lessen the workload impact of performing backups?

There is perhaps no greater responsibility for the database administrator than establishing proper backup and recovery plans. Although the DBA performs other important tasks, nothing approaches the critical nature of ensuring the protection of key corporate data. For this reason, great pains should be taken to ensure that a customized backup and recovery plan is put in place for each critical database. In addition, the master should ensure each customized plan is practiced on development servers to ensure each plan and disaster recovery scenario actually works. Not doing so can lead to ugly surprises if a true failure occurs.

 DBAs can work hard at performance tuning and be renowned for optimizing a server, but if they are not practicing good backup strategies, they may likely be found without a job and with a tarnished reputation.

When it comes to data governed by Microsoft SQL Server, a DBA needs to, at a minimum, use the below checklist to ensure a proper backup and recovery plan is in place to protect key corporate data:

- Is there a customized plan in place for the database that addresses its specific data recovery needs?

- Is storage space used by backup files being conserved intelligently?

- Are backup files being secured to guard sensitive data?

- Is the backup plan set up in an automated fashion to reliably occur without DBA intervention?

- Is the DBA kept informed of backup activities, especially when a backup operation fails?

- Is there assurance the backup files are valid and can be used for recovery?

- Is everything possible being done to minimize the performance impact of backup operations?

- Can the DBA easily manage the backup/recovery strategy across all SQL Servers?

Each database has its own particular backup and recovery needs. Some static databases can get by on nightly full or differential backups, while a very dynamic and visible database might require a specialized point-in-time recovery plan. When mapping out a backup plan, the DBA needs to ascertain the recovery needs of a database from the application project leads that drive the overall system. Once determined, the DBA can then go about crafting a customized backup plan for the database.

SQL Server offers a number of different backup methods which allow a DBA to build a plan that exactly matches the recovery needs of the database. The basic backup methods include:

- **Full:** A complete, referentially intact, snapshot of the database is taken. This may be done while users continue to work on the system.

- **Differential:** A copy of all the pages in a database that have been modified since the last backup is made. Typically smaller than full backups, differential backups usually run quicker and have less performance impact on the system.

- **File/File Group:** For very large databases with high availability requirements, the DBA can intelligently split out various objects among certain files and file groups and only back up parts of a database when needed.

- **Transaction Log:** For systems requiring point-in-time recovery, backups are made of the transaction log at regular intervals. These backups can later be applied with Full or other backups to bring a database back to the last transaction log backup.

Now, the question of what can be done to minimize the performance impact of backups still pertains. This answer generally revolves around one's ability to reduce backup I/O in some form or fashion.

The first thing to be investigated for large databases that have long backup times is a plan to move from full backups to differential or file/file group backups. Differential backups will only backup data that has changed, so such routines should buy some reduced I/O. Also, if there is a large amount of stagnant data on a database, moving such data to specific files or file groups that do not require repetitive backups and then only backing up files or file groups with dynamically changing data can be considered.

Third party solutions offering backup software designed to reduce backup windows is also an option. Such software typically intercepts the Microsoft backup stream and applies some form of compression algorithm, so that the actual physical backup file is much smaller than its original size. It is not uncommon for such software to reduce backup sizes by 80-90%. Of course, such compression results in much less physical I/O. Not only are storage needs reduced, but the actual backup times shrink anywhere from 50-80%. Recovery times can also be lessened, although the maximum time reductions are usually only in the neighborhood of 50%.

Embarcadero Technologies and Idera offer such backup software. So, if a budget for software tools is available and large databases with elongated backup times are present, the trial of such software to see if it makes sense for the situation is advisable.

Proper Database and Log File Placement

Lastly, with respect to database I/O, the DBA should make sure the database and log files are on separate drives and the drives are formatted properly for the files' demands. For static databases, this might not be too much of an issue, but for dynamic databases, it is critical.

Separating database and log files help lessen the impact of physical I/O contention at the server level as long as separate controllers exist for the drives in question. Drive selection and formatting are important, too.

Log activity is obviously very write intensive, so RAID format selection makes a big difference in performance. RAID5 is not the natural choice for log or TEMPDB files, but RAID0, RAID1, RAID0+1, or RAID1+0 are good choices. RAID5 can be okay for database files, especially for read intensive databases.

Chapter 5 contains a procedure named *up_bn_storage_overview* that provides a good storage overview of SQL Server and specifically presents a listing of database and log placements on the server drives. This procedure instantly reveals if database and log files were accidentally placed on the same drive or other drives whose RAID levels are not right for the files in question.

After performing server and database workload analysis, the DBA can then begin to dive into session and SQL analysis, focusing on databases exhibiting the highest overall server workloads.

Session Workload Analysis

It has been correctly stated that databases would perform just fine if no users were ever allowed to log into them. Alas, this is never the case, so the SQL Server DBA will need to be able to identify the workload hogs on the server and figure out why they are using more resources than they should. A general rule of thumb is: if any user session is found using more than 25% of any resource (CPU, I/O, etc.), their SQL and usage patterns should be examined in more detail.

To start, it is a good idea to get a quick overview of how many sessions have been logged into SQL Server, along with counts of how many are active and inactive. The *sess_count* query below will accomplish this task:

🖫 sess_count.sql

```
-- Script is available in the Online Code Depot
```

The results will look like:

```
active_processes      inactive_processes      system_processes
----------------      ------------------      ----------------
1                     25                      15
```

From there, the DBA should pinpoint sessions using the lion's share of resources, as it is not uncommon for 10% of the session base to be causing severe pain for the other 90% of those trying to use SQL Server. There are two ways to view this type of data. A good way to accomplish this is to break out session usage by percentage, making it impossible for session hogs to escape notice. The following procedure, *up_wl_session_hogs*, makes this easy to accomplish:

💾 up_wl_session_hogs
```
-- Script is available in the Online Code Depot
```

Figure 7.5 is a representation of the query looking for session resource hogs.

	loadtype	spid	username	pctused
1	Top CPU Process	55	sa	51.23
2	Top I/O Process	60	sa	25.00
3	Top Memory Process	53	sa	27.22
4	Top Transaction Process	2	sa	.00

Figure 7.5: *Finding Session Hogs.*

Sessions on dynamic systems having accumulated more than 25% of one resource are candidates for further examination. Of course, large batch job processes that come and go at predefined intervals may not be a problem, but consistently connected sessions exhibiting high resource usage are another matter.

Of course, with SQL Server, it is easy to get the standard session analysis that gives a quick overview of what each session is doing. The *sess_activity* query provides everything needed to acquire more details on each process connected to SQL Server:

```
-- Script is available in the Online Code Depot
```

Figure 7.6 is a representation of the results of this query.

	spid	loginame	windows_user	database_name	status	program_name	mem_bytes	cpu	physical_io	blocked	hostname	open_tran	
1	1 sa			master	background		0	100	0	No		No	LAZY
2	2 sa			master	sleeping		0	0	0	No		No	LOG v
3	3 sa			master	background		48	10	0	No		No	SIGNA
4	4 sa			master	background		96	0	0	No		No	LOCK
5	5 sa			master	background		16	0	2	No		No	TASK
6	6 sa			master	background		16	0	0	No		No	TASK
7	7 sa			master	sleeping		0	0	23	No		No	CHEC
8	8 sa			master	background		16	0	0	No		No	TASK
9	9 sa			master	background		16	0	0	No		No	TASK
10	10 sa			master	background		16	0	0	No		No	TASK
11	11 sa			master	background		16	0	0	No		No	TASK
12	12 sa			master	background		16	0	5	No		No	TASK
13	13 sa			master	background		16	0	0	No		No	TASK
14	51 NT AUTHORITY\SYSTEM	SYSTEM		msdb	sleeping	SQLAgent - Generic Refresher	224	30	23	No	SFLRSCHM2	No	AWAI
15	52 NT AUTHORITY\SYSTEM	SYSTEM		msdb	sleeping	SQLAgent - Alert Engine	112	10743	5	No	SFLRSCHM2	No	AWAI
16	53 sa			master	sleeping	Perf Analyst	440	13614	21	No	SFLRSCHM2	No	AWAI
17	54 sa			master	sleeping	DBArtisan	0	0	0	No	SFLRSCHM2	No	AWAI
18	55 sa			master	sleeping	Perf Analyst	160	26251	0	No	SFLRSCHM2	No	AWAI
19	56 sa			master	sleeping	Perf Analyst	0	40	0	No	SFLRSCHM2	No	AWAI
20	57 sa			master	runnable	Perf Analyst	8	60	0	No	SFLRSCHM2	No	SELEC
21	58 sa			master	sleeping	Embarcadero IntelliSense	0	40	0	No	SFLRSCHM2	No	AWAI
22	59 sa			master	sleeping	DBArtisan	16	30	0	No	SFLRSCHM2	No	AWAI
23	60 sa			master	runnable	DBArtisan	200	181	24	No	SFLRSCHM2	No	SELEC

Figure 7.6: *Viewing session details.*

The natural question to ask once a session is found that seems to be busy with activity is, "What the heck are they doing?" One simple approach to finding the answer is to issue a DBCC INPUTBUFFER command and pass in the SPID of interest. Quick output, the first 255 bytes, of the current/last SQL statement issued by the process will be returned. While some issues can be caught like this, it is much better to trace suspicious sessions.

"I See You!"

While being a DBA can be stressful, it can also be entertaining. One particularly amusing thing is shining the spotlight on a rogue user who swears up and down they are not doing anything affecting the system. There is something oddly enjoyable about proving that indeed they are wreaking havoc. While this may not be easy to do with certain database engines, it is quite easy to accomplish with SQL Server.

 Through tracing, literally every move a particular session or a whole group of users makes can be captured. There are a few things not available via a trace, like wait events a user session has experienced, but getting the issued SQL and the accompanying performance metrics should yield enough information to go on.

There are two basic methods for creating traces: using Microsoft's supplied SQL Profiling tool (SQL Profiler); and creating trace files on the server for later viewing, either through SQL Profiler or another interface. An upcoming section will explain why it is generally more efficient to create server side traces, but for now, both approaches will be reviewed, starting with the SQL Profiler.

For the purposes of this book, it is assumed the DBA has had some experience with the tool. Thus, this section will not go through every aspect of creating traces, templates, etc. Instead, it will focus on how to find out what a particular process is up to.

When a particular session is pinpointed through use of this chapter's queries or stored procedures, and yet a desire for more information remains, SQL Profiler should be opened and a new trace started. On the Filters tab of the Trace Properties dialog, for SQL Server versions 7 – 2000, scroll down to the SPID filter and enter in the SPID to be watched. Figure 7.7 below shows SQL Profiler used to trace a session in SQL Server 2000.

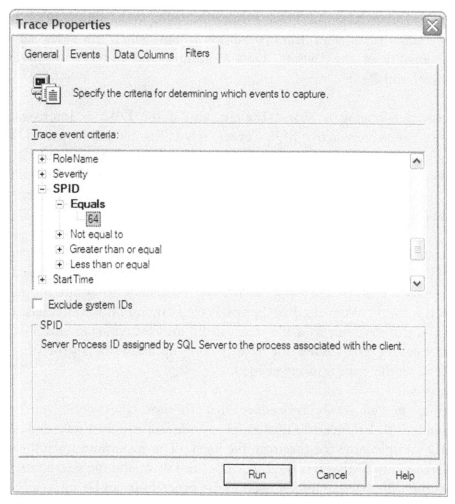

Figure 7.7: *Using Profiler to trace a particular session in SQL Server 2000.*

The events the DBA will want to acquire nearly always include the Stored Procedure RPC:Completed and SP:StmtCompleted events. These allow the DBA to catch stored procedure executions and the individual T-SQL statement calls within them along with the TSQL SQL:BatchCompleted event. Once the SPID filter and the events are set, one simply clicks OK on the Trace Properties dialog and the process begins.

In SQL Server 2005, the Trace Properties dialog looks a little different in that there is only an Events Selection tab which provides all the functionality of the Events, Data Columns, and Filters tabs in SQL Server 7 and 2000.

Server side tracing is more efficient, and if the DBA is interrogating sessions on a very active SQL Server, this is the avenue to use. DBAs have different styles of performing server side tracing, but one of the easiest ways is to create one or more stored procedures that contain all the trace properties, which are fed the SID to be tracked along with a trace file name to be written to on the server.

Personal stored procedures can be written for tracing or SQL Profiler can be allowed to do most of the work and the code massaged as necessary. One of the options in SQL Profiler is to script the trace, which is found under the File\Script Trace... menu option that has been built in the tool, out to a file that can be invoked via standard T-SQL. This way, the DBA does not have to look up and code all the obscure calls to set the trace options needed.

The *up_wl_trace_session* procedure that follows takes code generated through SQL Profiler and uses custom code to provide a way to pass in a SID and filename for the trace file itself. The maximum trace file size is defaulted to 5MB, so if the DBA does not want any file size limits, the maximum file size parameter used in the procedure can be set to a much larger amount.

🖫 up_wl_trace_session
-- Script is available in the Online Code Depot

The above procedure only starts a session trace, so when all the needed information needed has been received, the trace can be stopped by issuing the following two commands. These commands pass the trace number that has been received as output from the *up_wl_trace_session* procedure execution.

```
exec sp_trace_setstatus < input trace number >,0
exec sp_trace_setstatus < input trace number >,2
```

Once these commands complete, the trace can be viewed through SQL Profiler by using the Open Trace File option in the tool and selecting the trace file that was created.

Another option is to use the *fn_trace_gettable* function below to view trace results. Once the trace file is created, a SQL like the following can be issued to view the output, substituting the trace file name for the example one shown:

```
select
    *
from
    ::fn_trace_gettable
    ('c:\dev\trace\trace64.trc',default)
```

Once this point of tracing SQL for sessions has been reached, it is time to move into SQL workload analysis. This type of analysis concerns itself with examining SQL on a global, database, and session level.

SQL Workload Analysis

An interesting SQL story actually happened on a Teradata system and not a SQL Server, but it still demonstrates how important it is to find bad SQL, preferably before it is let loose on an unsuspecting database server.

"Bob" was a really nice guy but an absolute novice at writing SQL code. Bob was fresh out of computer science school and was hired at a large national insurance company.

The company maintained insurance claim information dating back to approximately the time of Noah's flood, so one can imagine the volume of data being managed. Because of this, the company purchased a very expensive and large Teradata system that served as the company's data warehouse. Bob was placed into a group of SQL developers that were charged with the task of writing decision support queries against the mammoth Teradata warehouse.

One day Bob asked the DBA group to look at a query he had written against the warehouse. It was truly an absolute monster.

If a DBA has never had the pleasure of working with Teradata, he has missed a treat because it is a database junkie's dream come true. Infinitely scalable architecture, massive parallel processors, tons of RAM, and fast hashing algorithms are used to distribute the tons of data among its many storage devices. Teradata also has a unique EXPLAIN plan that not only communicates the paths used to obtain a SQL result set, but also gives a time estimate of how long it believes the query will take to run.

Bob was asked if he had run his query through the EXPLAIN utility and he said, he had not. In fact did not know that such a thing existed. So without any other review of his query, it was put through an EXPLAIN. Teradata went through its computations and issued back a response. The year that this happened was 1993, and according to Teradata, Bob's query, if executed, would not finish until the year 2049.

This story is completely true and highlights how damaging SQL can be in untrained hands. Unfortunately, there are many SQL novices currently working in IT shops getting ready to submit "the big one," and their number is growing. Faced with a shortage of qualified database personnel, companies are throwing guys like Bob into the meat grinder and expecting them to write SQL code that meets the response time expectations of end users.

The DBA needs to have the right game plan in place for finding and fixing problem SQL code in the database. Fortunately, SQL Server is pretty good in terms of helping DBAs locate and analyze potentially bad SQL. By using the roadmap and scripts provided in this chapter, the DBA should be able make short work of pinpointing any bad SQL being run though the system.

What is Bad SQL?

Before the DBA can identify problem SQL in the database, the question of "What is bad SQL?" needs to be asked. What criteria should be used when the hunt for problem SQL in critical systems is performed?

Even seasoned experts disagree on what constitutes efficient and inefficient SQL, so there is no way to sufficiently answer this question to every Microsoft professional's satisfaction. The following list contains general criteria that can be used when evaluating the output from various database monitors or personal diagnosticScripts:

- **Overall Response (Elapsed) Time:** This is how much time the query took to parse, execute, and fetch the data needed to satisfy the query. It should not include the network time needed to make the round trip from the requesting client workstation to the database server.

- **CPU Time:** This is how much CPU time the query took to parse, execute, and fetch the data needed to satisfy the query.

- **Physical I/O:** Often used as the major statistic in terms of identifying good vs. bad SQL, this is a measure of how many disk reads were caused by the query in order to satisfy the user's request. While controlling disk I/O is desired, it is important the DBA not focus solely on physical I/O as the single benchmark of inefficient SQL. Make no mistake, disk access is slower than memory access and also consumes processing time making the physical to logical transition, but the entire I/O picture of a SQL statement should be considered. This includes looking at a statement's logical I/O as well.

- **Logical I/O:** This is a measure of how many memory reads the query took to satisfy the user's request. The goal of tuning I/O for a query should be to examine both logical and physical I/O and use appropriate mechanisms to keep both to a minimum.

- **Repetition:** This is a measure of how often the query has been executed. A problem in this area is not as easy to spot as the others unless the DBA is very familiar with the application. A query that takes a fraction of a second to execute may still be causing a headache on the system if it is executed erroneously. One example would be a query that executes in a runaway T-SQL loop over and over again.

There are other criteria that can be examined. Examples include criteria such as sort activity, temp table usage, or access plan statistics that show items such as Cartesian joins and the like; however, more often than not, these measures are reflected in the criteria listed above. Fortunately, SQL Server records most of the above measures. This makes tracking the SQL that has been submitted against Microsoft databases much easier than other database engines.

System Waste

A number of database gurus are beginning to sound the alarm about a new type of SQL-related problem, one that has been given the name, *system waste*. Just what is system waste? The definition is any code run on the database server that does not add value to the business.

Experts claim there is a lot of code being run in database-driven applications that does not, for example, cause purchase orders to be printed faster or deliver customer information to online users any better. It is code that simply uses up CPU cycles and competes for I/O resources that true business-related logic could take advantage of.

Such code can be difficult to find, but there is definitely value in going through the exercise. Eliminating code that runs very fast is still worthwhile because the most efficient query *will always be the one that has not been run* or has to run!

Back up for a moment and return to the issue at hand; how to perform SQL workload analysis in general. There are some global factors to consider when using this method. The next section will begin with global factors. It will then move into capturing and examining individual SQL statements and stored code executions.

Global SQL Metrics

When performing SQL workload analysis, there are not many global SQL metrics to examine. However, the ones SQL Server makes available certainly deserve a cursory review. The *global_sql* query below will easily pick these up:

🖫 global_sql
```
-- Script is available in the Online Code Depot
```

The main two metrics of interest are failed auto-params and SQL re-compilations. Auto-parameterization occurs when an instance of SQL Server attempts to reuse a cached plan for a previously executed query similar to, but not the same as, the current query. The failed auto-param metric shows the number of failed auto-parameterization attempts.

SQL Server's ability to match new SQL statements with existing, unused execution plans increases when parameters or parameter markers are used in T-SQL statements. If a SQL statement is executed without parameters, SQL Server parameterizes the statement internally to increase the possibility of matching it against an existing execution plan.

A small number for this statistic shows SQL Server is efficiently reusing existing cached plans. The ability of SQL Server to match complex SQL statements to existing, unused execution plans, can be increased by explicitly specifying the parameters using either *sp_executesql* or parameter markers in the T-SQL code. Doing this helps lower the number of failed auto-parameterizations.

The SQL re-compilations statistic represents the total number of recompiles triggered in a SQL Server instance. Recompiles occur when SQL Server determines the currently defined execution plan for an executing stored procedure might no longer be the best possible plan. SQL Server pauses the query execution and recompiles the stored procedure.

Recompiles slow down the process executing the procedure and increase the load on the CPU. Further, the procedure will place a compile lock on the objects referenced by the code, which may increase the risk of lock contention on the system.

By extension, the more recompiles occurring on the system, the more overall load increases resulting in poor performance. In general, the number of recompiles should be kept low. The most common reasons SQL Server would issue a recompile are:

- Running *sp_recompile* against any table referenced in the stored procedure.

- Significant data changes in a referenced table.

- Schema changes to referenced objects.

- The use of the WITH RECOMPILE clause in the CREATE PROCEDURE or EXECUTEstatement when a plan is no longer available in the system cache.

- Use of tempoary objects in certain circumstances.

- Setting certain options to a non-default setting (OFF). These include *ansi_defaults, ansi_nulls, ansi_padding, ansi_warnings,* and *concat_null_yeilds_null.*

The DBA can locate stored procedures causing recompiles by setting traces either through SQL Profiler or server side traces and can catch the Stored Procedures SP:Recompile event.

The individual SQL statements causing the recompile can sometimes be discovered by collecting the SP:StmtStarting and SP:StmtCompleted events. SQL statements appearing immediately before and after the recompile event are the culprits.

SQL Statement Analysis

While it might not be true that 80% or more of a database server's performance is derived from the code that runs inside it with physical design as the number one contributor to performance, one or more bad SQL statements can certainly affect SQL Server's speed at servicing requests. Therefore, it is important the DBA stay on top of what SQL is issued on the servers and be very adept at ferreting out problematic SQL statements and stored procedures.

Primary attributes used when determining whether or not a particular set of SQL or a stored procedure is worth looking into as well as tuning have already been covered. So, the question is, "How does the DBA find such code?" Unlike some database engines such as Oracle, SQL Server 7 and 2000 do not have dynamic query views that contain issued SQL statements and their execution statistics.

In SQL Server 2005, a new view, *sys.dm_exec_query_stats* appears to contain performance execution statistics for issued SQL. As of this writing, it appears the best way to get usable information is to issue a query such as the following *sql_stats_2005.sql* script:

sql_stats_2005.sql

```
-- Script is available in the Online Code Depot
```

Figure 7.8 is a representation of the results of the above query run to look into SQL execution metrics.

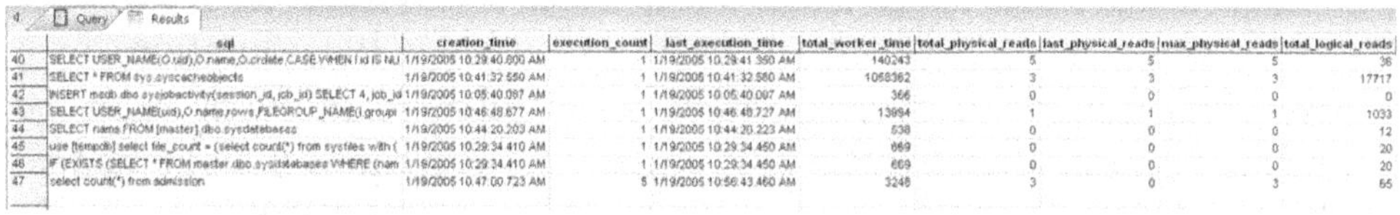

	sql	creation_time	execution_count	last_execution_time	total_worker_time	total_physical_reads	last_physical_reads	max_physical_reads	total_logical_reads
40	SELECT USER_NAME(O.uid),O.name,O.crdate,CASE WHEN I.id IS NU	1/19/2005 10:29:40.600 AM	1	1/19/2005 10:29:41.390 AM	140243	5	5	5	36
41	SELECT * FROM sys.syscacheobjects	1/19/2005 10:41:32.550 AM	1	1/19/2005 10:41:32.580 AM	1068362	3	3	3	17717
42	INSERT msdb.dbo.sysjobactivity(session_id, job_id) SELECT 4, job_id	1/19/2005 10:05:40.097 AM	1	1/19/2005 10:05:40.097 AM	366	0	0	0	0
43	SELECT USER_NAME(uid),O.name,rows,FILEGROUP_NAME(i.groupi	1/19/2005 10:46:48.677 AM	1	1/19/2005 10:46:48.727 AM	13994	1	1	1	1033
44	SELECT name FROM [master].dbo.sysdatabases	1/19/2005 10:44:20.203 AM	1	1/19/2005 10:44:20.223 AM	538	0	0	0	12
45	use [tempdb] select file_count = (select count(*) from sysfiles with (	1/19/2005 10:29:34.410 AM	1	1/19/2005 10:29:34.450 AM	669	0	0	0	20
46	IF (EXISTS (SELECT * FROM master.dbo.sysdatabases WHERE (nam	1/19/2005 10:29:34.410 AM	1	1/19/2005 10:29:34.450 AM	669	0	0	0	20
47	select count(*) from admission	1/19/2005 10:47:00.723 AM	5	1/19/2005 10:56:43.460 AM	3246	3	0	3	65

Figure 7.8: *Examining SQL execution metrics in SQL Server 2005.*

The DBA may not see every query issued against the server in the above query because only cached statements and statistics will be shown. Therefore, whether using SQL Server 7, 2000 or 2005, the one concrete way of capturing code executed against the server is through the use of traces.

It is a fact that it is typically more efficient to use server side tracing, than to track issued SQL through the Microsoft SQL Profiler tool. In addition, for busy servers, it is usually not wise to collect trace data into a table whose data can be evaluated later. What are the reasons behind these claims?

For starters, tracing through the SQL Profiling tool can cause two separate traces to be created, one of which is sent to the server and the other to the Profiler tool itself. Obviously, this causes redundant work. Also, SQL Server has to send data back over the wire to the Profiler tool increasing overhead and network traffic.

As to why not trace to a table; for busy servers, a lot more physical I/O can be expected to occur as trace data must be written to the table, plus such activity will eat up transaction log space and time as well. Tracing to a file on the server is much more efficient as data is just sequentially appended as would occur in any other file-based log.

However, even if server side tracing is used, there are a few best practice rules that are good to live by. First, it is wise to set a maximum size on the trace file so a hard drive cramped for space would not be overrun.

Second, because the DBA is primarily on the hunt for resource-intensive SQL, it is smart to use filters limiting the collected SQL to only statements or code objects exceeding certain CPU, duration, or I/O thresholds, somewhat like MySQL's long query log. The only caveat offered here is that it is not uncommon for certain SQL statements that run very fast to still cause a problem on the server if they are executed more times than needed.

Finally, end times can be set for trace collections to stop. This way, the amount of collection time can be limited; therefore, the data written to the file is limited. This feature is very useful if, for example, the activities of a batch cycle run between 1:00 a.m. and 3:00 a.m. in the morning needs to be traced. The DBA simply schedules the time for the trace to start via SQL Agent or some other scheduling tool and allows the trace to gracefully expire when needed.

Creating Traces

Every DBA is going to have their own preferences as to what events they want to trace, as well as what columns they want to see in terms of statistical metrics. That said, the *up_wl_trace_sql* procedure below allows the DBA to capture the SQL executions likely needed (individual SQL executions, procedure runs, plus SQL calls from each procedure run) to obtain the majority of statistics desired; excluding Microsoft system operations (SQL Agent, etc.) and allowing filters to be set on CPU, Reads, and Duration.

🖫 up_wl_trace_sql
```
-- Script is available in the Online Code Depot
```

The procedure's one required input is a trace file name written to the server. The trace will have to be manually stopped with a couple of commands that require the trace number. This trace number is outputted when the above procedure is run. If, for example, the trace number was one, the following commands would need to be issued for the file to be closed and available for analysis:

```
exec sp_trace_setstatus 1,0
exec sp_trace_setstatus 1,2
```

Viewing Trace Information

Once these commands complete, the trace can be viewed through SQL Profiler by using the Open Trace File option in the tool and selecting the trace file created for this purpose.

Another option is to use the *fn_trace_gettable* function to view trace results. Once the trace file has been created, a SQL like the following can be issued to view the output, substituting the trace file name for the example one shown:

```
select
    *
from
    ::fn_trace_gettable
    ('c:\dev\trace\tracetest.trc',default)
```

The nice thing about trace data is it is granular in that each execution of a SQL statement is seen as its own atomic unit. The bad thing about trace data is it is granular in that each execution of a SQL statement is seen as its own atomic unit.

Contradictory? Not really. There are some analysis situations in which the DBA needs to see each individual run of a SQL statement even if it is executed 1,000 times. There are other times, however, when the DBA wants an aggregation of a trace file so it can be seen, for example, that a particular SQL statement was run 1,000 times. This helps troubleshoot situations in which a SQL statement runs very fast, but runs much more often than it should and is therefore eating away at resources.

Unfortunately, the DBA cannot use the *fn_trace_gettable* function and perform aggregations on the *TextData* column, which contains the actual SQL text because the column type is a *text* datatype. However, a table from the function where the *TextData* column is altered to be a long *varchar* column such as 3000 or so can be created. The DBA can then find out execution counts with a simple query like the following:

```
select
    TextData,
    count(*)
from
    tracetab
group by
    TextData
order by
    2 desc
```

Conclusion

Workload analysis is an excellent method to use for uncovering general resource usage as well as the resource hogs on a SQL Server that exist at the database, session and SQL levels. The last chapter in this book will deal with tuning techniques for many of the diagnostics presented in this chapter, so stay tuned for this information. However, attention can be turned to the last performance analysis technique that should be practiced; ratio analysis.

Ratio Analysis

Techniques for Quickly Getting a Bird's Eye View of Performance

While bottleneck and workload analysis should be the two primary weapons used for troubleshooting SQL Server performance, an arsenal would not be complete without the third performance methodology; ratio analysis. Ratio analysis has gotten bad press lately, but even if current articles or white papers proclaim this analytical method should be tossed away, one should carefully read this chapter to determine whether this currently maligned technique is really as bad as some believe.

What is Ratio Analysis?

Ratio-based analysis has been around for many years. It used to be the only technique database administrators employed when called upon to diagnose the cause of database slowdown. Using one or more cherished SQL scripts; the DBA would conduct an examination of key ratios such as database memory use, contention, I/O, network utilization, and others to pinpoint the area(s) responsible for unacceptable performance.

Once a particular area was identified as suspect, the standard remedy was to increase the resources for that area. This often did the trick but occasionally failed to produce any real performance gain.

Should ratio-based analysis still be used to assist in determining the overall health of a database, and if so, how should it be done?

When performed correctly, ratio-based analysis definitely has a place in the DBA's performance-tuning arsenal. Performance ratios are very good roll-up mechanisms for busy DBAs, making at-a-glance analysis possible.

Many DBAs have large database farms to contend with and cannot spend time checking detailed wait-based analysis outputs for every SQL Server they oversee. Succinct performance ratios can assist in such situations by giving DBAs a few solid indicators that can be scanned quickly to see if any database server requires immediate attention.

This chapter will present a number of scripts that calculate valuable ratios that can be used to get a handle on the performance of the database server.

Deficiencies of Only Using a Bottleneck Approach

Ratio-based analysis is still viable because a pure wait-based or bottleneck approach will miss a number of critical items that indicate poor performance. For example, the wait events in SQL Server do not do a very good job of identifying physical I/O access, but the buffer cache hit ratio does.

Accurate Ratio Analysis Techniques

How does one accurately perform ratio-based analysis? While there are certainly many opinions as to which rules to follow, some standards should always be adhered. To begin with, many formulas that make up ratio-based analysis must be derived from delta measurements instead of cumulative statistics, and this can be tough in SQL Server.

Many of the global ratios that a DBA will examine come from the *master.dbo.sysperfinfo* table. This table maintains a count of all occurrences in the *cntr_value* column of a particular database statistic since the server was brought up. For database servers kept up for long periods of time, these values can grow quite large and will impact how a particular ratio is interpreted.

For example, the buffer cache hit ratio was deemed fairly useless by Microsoft if a server had been up for a long time period. If SQL Server had been running for many weeks, the numbers representing the I/O statistics would likely be enormous. The counts of logical reads (memory reads) will be very large, and in most systems exceed the count of physical reads by a wide margin. Such a situation can, if it is computed solely with cumulative value counts, skew the buffer cache hit ratio.

If an inefficient query is issued causing many physical reads, adding them to the counters would probably not trigger a meaningful dip in the overall cache hit ratio, as long as cumulative statistics are used. However, if delta statistics are used, the portrayal of the cache hit ratio would be more current and accurate. Indeed, more recent versions of SQL Server now take into account only the last few thousand page reads when factoring the statistics that make up the ratio. Therefore, the measure has become more valuable.

Some ratios do not rely on *sysperinfo*, and as a result can be derived from current/cumulative values. One example of this is the blocking lock ratio. This lock ratio computes the percentage of user sessions currently blocked on a system. Because locks in a database are repeatedly obtained and released, the ratio can be computed with cumulative numbers from one performance view without the need for taking a before-and-after statistical snapshot.

In addition to using delta statistics to compute many of the key metrics in ratio-based performance analysis, DBAs must also be committed to examining all database categories that contribute to overall health and well-being. This can mean employing ratios and analytic percentages that have historically been neglected by DBAs.

For instance, many DBAs do not use ratios when examining their object structures in a database because they have not seen how such a technique can be applied to objects. However, ratio-based analysis can definitely be utilized to determine if objects such as tables and indexes are disorganized. For instance, finding the global percentage of tables containing forwarded rows may help a DBA realize he is not properly defining the table storage parameters in a dynamic database.

A final thing to remember about using ratio-based analysis is, while there are several rules of thumb that can be used as starting points in the evaluation of database performance, each database has an individual personality. Some hard and fast rules simply will not apply to every database.

For example, an e-commerce application never saw its cache hit ratio rise above 75%, a measure that would normally cause concern to most database analysts. Oddly enough, none of the routinely vocal users of the system ever complained, response times always appeared good, the SQL seemed well-tuned and adding more database buffers never seemed to improve the situation. For that particular database, 75% was the benchmark to use for gauging the efficiency of logical/physical I/O activity in the database server.

So, does ratio-based analysis still sound like old hat or can it potentially add value to a DBA's performance analysis toolkit? With a renewed appreciation of ratio-based analysis, the determination of which ratios will benefit DBAs in troubleshooting SQL Server performance can be explored. Many of the ratios and statistics revolve around memory usage and memory vs. physical I/O access, so this is a good place to start.

Memory Ratios

Most DBAs would fit all their key databases into RAM if they could, but alas, with database sizes growing at an average of 42% a year, this is not a viable option. So, DBAs and developers alike work to keep data access to a minimum and attempt to keep as much often-used data in memory as possible so response times remain low and acceptable.

In addition to keeping referenced data in memory, DBAs are becoming all too aware that keeping parse and compile activities of queries and code objects low plays a big part in performance. All database engines, including SQL Server, keep query and code plans in a cache, the Plan Cache, so identical requests for both code object and queries can avoid the sometimes lengthy parse process and proceed straight to execution helping runtime performance.

An exception to this rule applies when a procedure or query depends on parameters that are passed into it playing a part in how SQL Server should execute the request or affect the size of the result set. Whereas one plan may work great for a particular input parameter, another parameter may dramatically alter the result set returns and run much better with a different access plan.

SQL Server has offered dynamic memory management since version 7.0. This means the DBA can turn loose the reins and let SQL Server determine workload demands and adjust memory accordingly, with one eye always on overall server memory utilization, in order to keep performance high. The basic memory regions SQL Server uses are the database or buffer cache, the plan cache, referred to in older versions as the procedure cache, and workspace memory.

The database cache holds 8KB pages that contain database information. SQL Server attempts to eliminate seldom-used pages from the database cache so room is left for often-referenced data.

As has already been mentioned, the plan cache holds compiled and executable plans for both code objects (procedures, etc.) and ad-hoc queries.

Workspace memory is sometimes required for database requests that require hashing or sorting operations. There are also miscellaneous areas of memory used for locking and such.

Before looking at the various memory efficiency ratios, it is a good idea to understand how much memory SQL Server has allocated across the various memory regions. The *up_memory_status* procedure below works for SQL Server 2000 and 2005 and gives a quick overview of all primary memory allotments:

⊟ up_memory_status

```
-- Script is available in the Online Code Depot
```

Once the amount of memory SQL Server has allocated for use has been revealed, the DBA can then move on to looking at various memory efficiency ratios. The *up_ratios_memory* procedure should work on all versions of SQL Server. It returns the buffer cache, procedure plan, ad-hoc SQL, and log cache hit ratios:

⊟ up_ratios_memory

```
-- Script is available in the Online Code Depot
```

Looking at Buffer Cache Performance

To help ensure excellent performance, the buffer cache hit ratio should be maintained in the neighborhood of 90% or higher. However, one should be aware that every server has its own personality and might exhibit excellent performance with below average readings for the cache hit ratio. One should also be aware that excessive logical I/O activity can produce a very high cache hit ratio while actually degrading overall database performance, so a high buffer cache hit ratio is not the silver bullet for overall high performance in SQL Server.

If the DBA is seeing low readings for the buffer cache hit ratio, the Page Life Expectancy statistic should be checked. This statistic indicates the length of time SQL Server estimates a page will remain in the buffer cache. Obviously, pages served from memory result in much shorter response times than pages that must be read from disk and then into the cache. So, it is wise for often used data to be pinned in the buffer cache. The *page_life* query easily provides the DBA with this measure:

🖫 page_life.sql

```
-- Copyright © 2005 by Rampant TechPress
-- This script is free for non-commercial purposes
-- with no warranties.  Use at your own risk.
--
-- To license this script for a commercial purpose,
-- contact info@rampant.cc
-- ***************************************************

select
    cntr_value
from
    master..sysperfinfo
where
    object_name = 'SQLServer:Buffer Manager' and
    counter_name = 'Page life expectancy'
```

Page life expectancy readings of 300 seconds or less often indicate too many table scans are occurring which is an activity that can flood the buffer cache with pages used only once or seldom, at best. Checking the I/O access patterns with scripts provided in the prior section can confirm excessive scan activity.

SQL Server tends to be either data-centric or code-centric. Most servers are data-centric, meaning memory is dominated by requested data pages. This can be verified with the *data_centric* query:

🖫 data_centric.sql

```
-- Script is available in the Online Code Depot
```

Any ratio over 50% in the above query signifies a server is data-centric in nature. One caveat is that a high reading may also indicate excessive large table scans. That is something that can be confirmed by checking the page life expectancy metric.

The DBA can take a peek into the objects in the buffer cache for SQL Server 7 and 2000 using the DBCC MEMUSAGE(NAMES) command. This command supplies the top twenty objects in the buffer cache; however, it has been removed in SQL Server 2005.

Examining the Plan Cache

Attention can now focus on the procedure plan hit ratio. A high procedure cache hit rate is a desirable thing; the DBA should strive for a hit ratio between 95% - 100%, with 95% being a good performance benchmark for code reference.

When a database is first started, the procedure cache hit rate will not be at an optimal level because all code being used will be relatively new, must be read in from disk, and placed into the cache. If, however, after a solid hour or two of steady database time, the procedure cache hit rate has not increased to desirable levels, the DBA should look into increasing the amount of memory given to SQL Server.

Plan reuse can backfire since input parameters are capable of causing drastic changes in returned result sets. One set of bind/input parameters could produce an end result set that works well with a particular access path, but that same path may produce terrible response times for a different set of bind parameters.

Peering into the cache is not difficult. A simple query from the *master.dbo.syscacheobjects* table using the *plan_objects.sql* code is all that is needed:

🖫 plan_objects.sql
```
-- Script is available in the Online Code Depot
```

Figure 8.1 is a representation of a look into the plan object cache.

---

	objtype	cacheobjtype	objid	database_name	uid	usecounts	sqlbytes	sql	mem_kb
1	Proc	Compiled Plan	302624121	master	1	2	32	sp_sproc_columns	336
2	Proc	Compiled Plan	302624121	master	1	1	32	sp_sproc_columns	328
3	Proc	Compiled Plan	302624121	master	1	1	32	sp_sproc_columns	328
4	Proc	Compiled Plan	2021582240	master	1	1	26	sp_helprotect	256
5	Proc	Compiled Plan	2021582240	master	1	2	26	sp_helprotect	232
6	Proc	Executable Plan	302624121	master	1	1220	32	sp_sproc_columns	216
7	Proc	Executable Plan	302624121	master	1	2	32	sp_sproc_columns	216
8	Proc	Executable Plan	302624121	master	1	2	32	sp_sproc_columns	216
9	Proc	Executable Plan	302624121	master	1	2	32	sp_sproc_columns	216
10	Proc	Compiled Plan	194099732	master	1	1	18	sp_rename	208
11	Proc	Compiled Plan	75863337	master	1	1	56	sp_embt_pa_space_bottlenecks	184
12	Proc	Compiled Plan	2037582297	master	1	2	22	sp_helptext	176
13	Proc	Compiled Plan	139863565	master	1	1	56	sp_embt_pa_database_analysis	176
14	Proc	Compiled Plan	1999346187	master	1	1	60	sp_embt_pa_home_storage_totals	160
15	Proc	Compiled Plan	2079346472	master	1	1	54	sp_embt_pa_memory_ratio_mem	136
16	Proc	Compiled Plan	443864648	master	1	1	54	sp_embt_pa_io_hottest_files	136
17	Proc	Executable Plan	2037582297	master	1	1	22	sp_helptext	112
18	Proc	Compiled Plan	325576198	msdb	1	1	58	sp_sqlagent_get_perf_counters	104
19	Proc	Compiled Plan	261575970	msdb	1	1	58	sp_sqlagent_has_server_access	88
20	Proc	Compiled Plan	1967346073	master	1	1	54	sp_embt_pa_home_bottlenecks	80
21	Proc	Compiled Plan	46623209	master	1	1	32	sp_datatype_info	72
22	Proc	Compiled Plan	46623209	master	1	1	32	sp_datatype_info	72

Figure 8.1: *Examining the plan object cache.*

The output from the plan object cache query will provide not only the object and query names/text, but it will also reveal information such as how many times the code object or object structure was referenced, how much memory it is taking up, and etc.

Ad-hoc SQL requests will also be seen in the cache as well. The ad-hoc SQL hit ratio will tell how often general query plans are being reused. A high ad hoc hit rate is desirable, but is harder to maintain at a high level than something like a procedure cache hit rate. Therefore, an 80% or greater ad hoc cache hit rate is a good performance benchmark for code reference.

After first starting a database, it may take an hour or two of steady database time before the ad hoc hit rate will approach optimal levels. This occurs because all code being used is new, must be read in from disk, and then placed into the cache. However, if after this period of time the ad hoc cache hit rate has not reached a desirable level, the DBA should consider increasing the amout of memory given to the SQL Server.

Total vs. Target Memory

The previously covered memory ratios certainly help identify memory insufficiencies on the SQL Server, but there is one other set of metrics to be reviewed. This set of metrics is known as the Total vs. Target memory ratio query; *mempressure.sql*. This query presents the amount of total memory SQL Server is currently using vs. the maximum amount of memory it could be using.

🖫 mempressure.sql
```
-- Script is available in the Online Code Depot
```

The results of the query will look like the following:

```
total_mem_mb          target_mem_mb  pressure_ratio
------------          -------------  ------------------------------
33                    318            10.40
```

SQL Server will dynamically adjust its memory allocations depending on workload up to either the maximum amount of memory configured by the DBA or the maximum memory it thinks it should use while giving consideration to other non-SQL Server Server activities.

If one sees the total memory approach or hit the target amount of defined memory, SQL Server is experiencing memory pressure. Adding more RAM to the machine or adjusting any memory ceiling limits imposed at the SQL Server configuration level may help.

Storage Ratios

Ratios can be useful in examining storage because they help put the true picture in perspective in terms of how space is being used or the state of a particular object. The primary ratios of value are:

- **Database and Log Used:** This ratio states how full a database or log is in terms of percent used.

- **Object Fragmentation:** This ratio states that logical, extent, and average fragmentation levels are always viewed as the percentage of fragmentation present.

- **Forwarded Rows:** This ratio states that knowing a table has 100 forwarded rows is not too useful, but knowing 97% of a table's rows are forwarded reveals to the DBA that reorganization is on the horizon for the table.

Chapter 5 of this book contains a number of stored procedures to help the DBA evaluate all of the above ratios. It should be read thoroughly to learn how those statistics are produced and evaluated.

Session Ratios

Ratio analysis can help the DBA get a handle on SQL Server session activity, what the top resource hogs are, how users are accessing database objects and how bad a case of lock contention is.

To get a session activity ratio, the *active_ratio* query below should be used:

active_ratio
```
-- Script is available in the Online Code Depot
```

The results will look like the following:

```
active_processes    inactive_processes    active_pct
----------------    ------------------    -------------------
1                   23                    4.35
```

A low activity ratio is a clue that many sessions are sitting idle and are eating up connection memory and other resources.

The previous chapter showed how to locate session resource hogs by using the *up_wl_session_hogs* procedure. Seeing resource usage amounts tied to individual sessions is a powerful way to identify processes that need more investigation.

---

	loadtype	spid	username	pctused
1	Top CPU Process	55	sa	51.23
2	Top I/O Process	60	sa	25.00
3	Top Memory Process	53	sa	27.22
4	Top Transaction Process	2	sa	.00

Figure 8.2: *Checking session resource usage ratios.*

Of course, many resource issues can be traced back to bad SQL and/or bad access paths. SQL Server does keep track of scans, index searches, etc., so by using the *access_ratios* query below, one can quickly determine if there are any issues with excessive scan activity:

access_ratios

```
-- Script is available in the Online Code Depot
```

Finally, many DBAs like to see ratios when examining blocking lock activity rather than raw block/lock counts, as it is sometimes better to know 90% of lock requests are waiting versus viewing straight numeric counts of blocks. The *block_ratio* query below provides just the information these DBAs are seeking:

block_ratio

```
-- Script is available in the Online Code Depot
```

In SQL Server 2005, the *sys.dm_tran_locks* view can be used in place of *syslockinfo* view.

Conclusion

Ratio analysis rounds out the three performance methodologies the DBA needs to use when monitoring SQL Servers for performance issues. Though the least important of the three, ratio analysis still provides valuable insights into the total SQL Server performance picture and makes it possible to understand quick facts relating to performance that will clue the DBA in to which servers need immediate attention.

With the discussion of the top performance monitoring methodologies complete, attention can now be turned to an area that is neglected by many DBAs. This neglect is such a crime because it is vital for administrators who want to be proactive in their work to understand the use of capacity planning. Capacity planning may not be easy to execute in the beginning, but once learned, will be used many times.

Performance Lifecycle Management: Steps 3 and 4

CHAPTER

9

Using History to Prepare for the Future

At one time or another, the following questions have very likely plagued the minds of many DBAs:

- How much storage will SQL Server need six months from now?

- How fast is the Enterprise Resource Planning (ERP) database growing?

- Which objects are responsible for the growth in the database?

- Will the new index added recently do any good?

- Will the server be able to support another instance of SQL Server?

- Is the performance of the database server getting better, staying the same, or getting worse?

These questions are nearly impossible to answer unless proper capacity planning techniques are practiced. Simply put, the process of capacity planning involves using today's information to predict tomorrow's needs.

When performed correctly, capacity planning helps reduce the overall cost of database ownership and maximizes the return on SQL Server investment. Thus, the end goal of capacity planning is to trim any future outages or slowdowns from the managed SQL Servers, along with trimming expenses from the company's bottom line.

In addition to seeking answers to the questions posed above, why should the DBA go to the trouble and time to institute capacity planning in the IT shop? How does one build a capacity planning system? This chapter will examine these questions to determine why capacity planning is necessary and will provide the techniques needed to design it correctly so that true and substantial benefits can be realized.

Why Perform Capacity Planning?

There are several reasons why the DBA should institute a capacity planning process. These reasons are listed as follows:

- The explosive growth of corporate data necessitates better data management to avoid storage-related outages and performance problems.

- The growing ratio of databases/servers managed per DBA has forced many DBAs to work in reactive instead of proactive mode, resulting in poor resource management.

- The interleaving of online application functions with backup and other important batch jobs requires that enough horsepower be available to handle many functions at once.

- Tight IT budgets mandate intelligent spending for new resources as well as the smart use of existing hardware resources and software licenses.

According to recent studies by IDC, a well known industry analyst group, the amount of enterprise data doubles roughly every two years. While this growth rate sounds high, it is actually conservative for some. For example, some Embarcadero customers are experiencing much higher growth rates. A conversation with one of their largest clients revealed that this particular client experienced a 166% data growth rate in their distributed database area last year.

Another company managing over 700 databases was expecting to take on another 300 databases by year end. With such high data growth rates, capacity planning becomes very important. Only by tracking the usage and historical growth patterns of data, along with actual performance ups and downs, will DBAs be able to accurately predict what their storage and performance needs will be in the future.

 Of course, high data growth presents challenges in addition to ensuring that enough raw storage exists to handle future loads. More data often equates to performance management headaches. A database with a history of performing adequately with a moderate amount of data may begin to produce unacceptable response times for a particular application when its data volume doubles or triples.

Such instances often require a review of the database's indexing scheme. Yet, through this review some DBAs find themselves shooting in the dark with respect to knowing whether adding indexes will actually do any good. However, capacity planning functions allow DBAs to better plan indexes by collecting index-based I/O measurements and access patterns. These measurements and patterns can then be reviewed to help determine the effectiveness of different indexing schemes. In essence, this is the same approach that Microsoft takes in its Index Tuning Wizard in SQL Server 7, SQL Server 2000 and the Database Tuning Component of SQL Server 2005.

In addition, the DBA facing growing amounts of data will also struggle with how to intelligently perform database and/or object reorganizations. High-growth databases tend to produce tough reorganization decisions in terms of knowing exactly what to reorganize and when. It is not smart to blindly reorganize all objects, as large tables and indexes can take an inordinate amount of time to rebuild. Whether done online or not, resources are required from the database to rebuild objects. This can be taxing to a system already straining against a growing data load. It is best if the DBA knows exactly what objects need to be reorganized and when, so that only necessary work is actually performed.

One way to determine such things is through an enforcement of reorganization thresholds. Thus, reorganization is only performed when an object actually needs it. Another method involves using trend analysis/capacity planning to see how fast objects fragment and break down. Such analysis also helps the DBA be proactive in the setting of *fillfactor*s for indexes and such.

Another reason capacity planning is necessary revolves around the fact that DBAs are managing more databases than ever. At Embarcadero, there is an average of 20-24 database servers managed per DBA, but that ratio can go much higher. The Embarcadero customer mentioned earlier who is currently utilizing 700 databases only has 15 DBAs to manage them, giving a ratio of nearly 47 to one!

Such high workloads result in the DBA's inability to stay familiar with the storage and resource consumption of the databases. When there are hundreds or thousands of SQL Server databases to keep track of, it is difficult to remember what is growing, what is not, and what needs performance assistance. An automated capacity planning process allows the DBA to relax and periodically review trend analysis, make forecasts for critical systems, and thus, act in a more proactive fashion.

Another area that is becoming more important is tracking the results of backup operations and their eventual outcomes, as well as other jobs. Often, DBAs try to time backup and batch job windows around the stopping and starting of underlying applications. Even with the online backup capabilities of SQL Server, large backups can still consume serious resources on a server, and because of this, DBAs like to keep backup times to a minimum. DBAs can use capacity planning to track backup and batch job times, and then utilize trend analysis to predict if times are staying flat or are increasing.

The final reason capacity planning makes sense is purely financial in nature. Although IT spending is increasing, most purchasing decisions are still heavily scrutinized and require fact-based justifications. Through

---

capacity planning, a DBA can deliver projections to an IT manager that can result in budget dollars being allocated for future needs.

In addition, many shops institute charge back for items such as database storage used, server capacity, etc. Capacity planning functions can deliver all the information necessary to determine factors such as the monthly storage percentage increases that certain databases have experienced and the amount of CPU resources that various applications are consuming on a server.

These and other reasons are catching the attention of third party software vendors as well as the database vendors themselves. In fact, one of the best features of the Oracle10g release was a bundled repository and built-in collection mechanism. This allows Oracle DBAs to easily collect and analyze historical performance and SQL execution patterns. Unfortunately, such features are not automated in SQL Server, so the DBA will have to develop an individual plan and management system.

Proper Capacity Planning Techniques

If the conclusion has been reached that a capacity planning process should be instituted, the next question is "How does the DBA build one?" Unfortunately, it is not easy to manually build a good capacity planning system, which is why most DBAs turn to third-party software vendors for help.

Microsoft provides a download on the main download site (www.microsoft.com/downloads) called the SQL Server Health and History Tool (SQLH2). This tool will provide a trend analysis starting point. With it, a DBA can get good, basic information like server uptimes, configuration settings, and some performance metrics. If there is no capacity planning system currently installed, it's definitely worth a try.

If Microsoft's free system is not robust enough for the current environment, then the DBA will need to create their own. The tasks involved in building a good capacity planning system generally revolve around the following steps:

- Designing a repository to hold one or more database's statistics.

- Building metric collection scripts.

- Intelligently scheduling metric collection scripts.

- Building analysis scripts.

- Formatting analysis output.

- Building forecasting scripts.

- Formatting forecasting output.

Although such tasks are not simple in nature and often explain why a DBA does not perform capacity planning, good tools do exist that make short work of the steps outlined above. However, a DBA who is unable to purchase such tools can still build a good capacity planning routine through a little upfront planning and diligent work.

For the DBA who is in the unfortunate rank of those who are required to build their own capacity planning system or is charged with evaluating third party vendor's offerings for capacity planning software, the following section will present each stepping stone in a process to be used to demonstrate what is required for a proper setup.

Obviously, capacity planning completely depends on a repository that accepts and contains collected historical statistics, as well as allowing structured and ad-hoc reporting for trend analysis and forecasting purposes. As with creating any database, a repository database can be designed in many different ways and its design depends on the need, scope, and scale of the proposed capacity planning system. However, there are a few must-have features any capacity planning repository must support.

First, the repository must be able to support more than one SQL Server database, as well as more than one physical SQL Server. If the organization is cross-platform in nature, meaning that the DBA supports more than one database vendor, it is good to design a repository that can manage different database platforms.

Enterprise-wide capacity planning means having the ability to zoom in or out on the entire database infrastructure. For this reason, a repository designed to work on just one server or platform may provide good information on a local level but fail to deliver the big picture that data center managers and IT directors are looking for.

Next, the repository must be set up to hold both scalar and result set data. This means it must be able to accept a single metric such as the buffer cache hit ratio, along with result set metrics such as a listing of SQL Server wait events or storage metrics for all databases on a server.

Of course, all metrics are collected multiple times over specific time periods, so the repository will need to manage iterations of collected statistics.

Speaking of time, the repository should support trouble-free purge ability, meaning a DBA should be able to easily keep, for example, only the last six months worth of data or whatever volume might be needed for their organization. Smart referential integrity planning makes such a thing usually simple to do.

Lastly, it is good if the repository can serve as a hub for all statistical collection metadata such as when collections started and stopped, which failed, etc. This provides one place to review instead of many when it comes to checking the progress of the capacity planning system.

Collecting Statistics

As the DBA begins to work through the process of building a SQL Server capacity planning system, the question may arise, "What exactly should be collected?" The answer to this question can vary widely depending on what one wants to track, analyze, and forecast.

As a general rule of thumb, the DBA should collect availability statistics, both global and object level storage-related measures and global, session and sometimes SQL level system usage/performance metrics.

On the availability front, the DBA is basically looking for heartbeats in the following areas:

- Up/down status of database server machine.

- Up/down status of SQL Server instance.

- Up/down status of SQL Server agent, if used for job scheduling, etc.

- Up/down status of miscellaneous and ancillary SQL Server components.

From a storage and object structure standpoint, some of the metrics that should be collected or tracked include the following:

- Database server-drive used and free space.

- Database total, used, free, and used/free percentages.

- Transaction log total, used, free, and used/free percentages.

- Database total table and index reserved space.

- Full database backup space used.

- Filegroup total, used, free, and used/free percentages.

- Total table and index reserved space for filegroups.

- File total size.

- Table and index reserved space.

- Table row counts.

- Table extent fragmentation (SQL 7 and 2000).

- Table logical fragmentation (SQL 7 and 2000).

- Table forwarded records.

- Table scan density (SQL 7 and 2000).

- Table average page density.

- Table extent count vs. extent switches (SQL 7 and 2000).

- Index extent fragmentation (SQL 7 and 2000).

- Index logical fragmentation (SQL 7 and 2000).

- Index scan density (SQL 7 and 2000).

- Average index fragmentation (SQL Server 2005).

When looking at what to collect from a performance standpoint, there are obviously several metrics that can be obtained from the *master.dbo.sysperfinfo* table as well as other sources. Table 8.1 lists some of the more important statistics that assist with trend analysis in their respective areas:

CATEGORY	STATISTIC
Memory	Buffer Cache Hit Ratio
	Procedure Plan/Cache Hit Ratio
	Ad-Hoc SQL Hit Ratio
	Free Cache Percent
	Page Life Expectancy
	Total Server Memory
	Target Server Memory
	Buffer Cache Size
	Plan Cache Size
	Latch Waits/Sec
I/O	Page Reads
	Page Writes
	Readahead Pages

CATEGORY	STATISTIC
	Log Flushes
	I/O Busy (@@IO_BUSY)
	Lazy Writes
	Extents Allocated
	Page Splits
	Bulk Copy Rows (global and by database)
	Bulk Copy Throughput (global and by database)
	Backup/Restore Throughput
	Forwarded Record Calls
	Full Scans
	Index Searches
	Probe Scans
	Range Scans
	File I/O (SQL 2000 and higher)
User Activity	Active Processes
	Inactive Processes
	CPU Busy (@@CPU_BUSY)
	Idle (@@IDLE)
	Transactions
	Locks
	Blocked Processes
	Deadlocks
	SQL Recompilations
	SQL Compilations
	Failed auto-params
Wait Events	All Events plus wait count and wait time
Server	Memory: Available Bytes
	Memory: Pages/sec
	Physical Disk: Avg. Disk Queue Length
	Physical Disk: Current Queue Length
	Processor: % Processor Time
	Processor: %User Time
	System: Processor Queue Length

Table 8.1: *Trend statistics*

If the DBA is going the extra mile to collect SQL statement metrics and trend them, the following list of statistics should be kept:

- SQL Statement
- Database
- Total Reads
- Total Writes
- Executions (derived)
- Total Elapsed Time
- Total CPU Time
- Execution Time

Delta vs. Static Values

When collecting various statistics, a decision needs to be made as to which statistics are to be delta-based and which metrics are to be cumulative in nature. For example, the Page Reads I/O statistic lends itself to being a delta-based measurement. The DBA should see the differences between the statistics each time an episode is captured. Other statistics, such as current blocked users, obviously will not be delta-based.

For delta-based statistics, the DBA should make sure algorithms are either built into the collection system so statistics are automatically converted into delta measures before they enter the capacity planning repository, or that the trend analysis front end/analysis scripts perform the delta math when reading cumulative numbers out of the repository.

Active vs. Passive Monitoring

Up until now, this book has been addressing passive monitoring through tracking statistics and running diagnostics on activities produced by the user community. In addition to passive monitoring, there is another form of monitoring finding favor with proactive shops; active monitoring. Active monitoring takes the approach of simulating work: transactions; queries; DDL, etc; and recording the response times of that specific work.

The idea behind active monitoring is the establishment of a baseline of the length of time a particular piece of work should take and then periodically re-introduced to see if any performance deviations occur. If the DBA desires, active monitoring measurements can become a part of the statistics collected for capacity planning purposes.

An example of an active monitoring framework is the *sp_minibench* stored procedure below. Written by Tom Sager, it helps gauge the performance of several different types of activities and provides an overall benchmark of information that can be gathered and tracked over time.

🖫 **sp_minibench**
```
-- Script is available in the Online Code Depot
```

Scheduling Statistical Collections

Once a decision has been made as to which metrics are to be tracked and analyzed and which method should be used to accomplish the statistical collection, the DBA can then focus on how to schedule the collection intervals. This is dictated by the dynamics of the actual SQL Servers being tracked.

As an example, a very static system may need to collect storage metrics only once a week or at most once a day. Even a dynamic system might need storage measures collected only once in a twenty-four hour period. However, system usage and performance metrics are another matter. Certain measures may need to be collected once an hour or even once every half-hour.

In terms of the actual scheduling mechanism, SQL Server provides SQL Agent, which has proven to be a fairly reliable scheduling system. The combination of stored procedures, which do the actual statistical collection, along with scheduled executions through SQL Agent has proven to be good for statistical collections.

Centralizing Operations

If there are several servers being tracked for capacity planning purposes, there will be some challenges ahead. First, if using a central repository to hold statistics for enterprise SQL Server installation, a linked server will need to be set up on each of the monitored SQL Servers that allow connectivity to the central SQL Server repository. This way, collection procedures can all insert directly into the capacity planning repository.

An optional method is to use replication and periodically feed the central repository from collection tables that exist on each SQL Server. While this works fine, it is not as clean as using the linked server setup.

The second issue is how to monitor the progress of all collection jobs. Actually, this does not differ in the challenge of monitoring any enterprise job backup system such as all backup routines. Centralized job scheduling software can help, but there are workarounds in using each individualized SQL Agent installation.

Setting up Trend Analysis

Once meaningful data is being acquired on a regular basis, the DBA can then begin analyzing the data: looking back in time as well as projecting forward.

In terms of analyzing historical data, it becomes easy to answer many of the questions posed at the beginning of this chapter such as "How fast is the database growing?" If the DBA decides to go granular on the collections, a drill-down analysis can be performed to discover answers to questions such as, "What objects are responsible for the spike in growth?"

In terms of data presentation, if a third-party tool for capacity planning is not being used, a number of good 4GL tools on the market or even

Microsoft Excel can be utilized to perform much of the computations and comparisons. But, what type of ability should the DBA build into an individual capacity planning system or what features should a third party tool have?

There are four basic needs to account for. They are as follows:

- Timeframes

- Statistical Aggregation

- Metric Rollups

- Drill Down

For trend analysis, the DBA will always begin with a time period of interest for the review. It might be a week, a month or a couple of hours. The trend analysis system must be able to take in Start/Stop time periods. Another good option is the ability to feed in simple requests such as, "Calculate the last six month's worth of data from the current date."

Next, the DBA will need to be able to view data in various forms of aggregation. For example, one might want to see: the average number of reads over a certain time period; the maximum amount of space ever used in one of the *tempdb* databases for the month of January; and so on.

The ability to perform rollups of various statistics is also necessary. For example, Page Reads may be collected every hour on one SQL Server, but it may be necessary to view the data by day over a particular week. Rollup capabilities allow this task to be accomplished.

Finally, the ability to drill down helps the DBA get to the bottom of specific trends. For example, a particular database may appear to be growing at a much faster rate than all the others, but the reason is unknown. If the ability to zoom in and drill down to objects in that database exists, the tables responsible for the overall growth can be discovered.

There are other features that make for good trend analysis presentations, but for now, these four will help the DBA get started.

Correlating Statistics

Correlating various measures to understand true performance trends take practice. Plotting singular measures helps answer basic questions such as, which databases are growing in size or the time of day SQL Server experiences peak user load; however, the performance of statistical cross-referencing is where things get really interesting.

For instance, the DBA may wonder if SQL Server is performing properly during periods of peak I/O. This becomes easy to understand when physical I/O (page reads, writes, etc.) are plotted with the *iostall* metric or with metrics in SQL Server 2005 derived from the *fn_virtualfilestats* function call, which provides a number of excellent I/O statistics. Indications of heavy I/O activity with little rise in latency indicates things may be just fine on the SQL Server.

Calculating Rates

Calculating growth rates is important for the next area of capacity planning; forecasting. For example, the DBA may have a database currently adding 50MB of new space each day. This is nice to know, but it is perhaps more valuable to understand that the database is growing at one percent per day or 30+% a month.

Rate calculations can sometimes be difficult to accomplish on statistics that appear to spike and then crash. For instance, *tempdb* usage may rise and fall during the month, but over time it may be steadily going up. The rate calculations must be able to smooth out the extremes so a reasonable rate of growth or decline can be calculated.

Predicting the Future

Prediction is a tougher nut to crack as the calculations involved can get complicated depending on what the DBA is trying to accomplish. Yet, sound predictions can be accomplished with a little mathematical research. Performed correctly, forecasting is where capacity planning really shines, as it helps the DBA act in a more proactive way. It also aids management in making intelligent budgeting decisions based on accurately forecasted future needs.

The next section, written by Tom Sager, covers how the DBA could go about building an individual capacity planning system. Tom is far and away superior at mathematics, so thanks to him for volunteering to handle this!

A Simple Example

As a way to demonstrate the capacity planning principles described in this chapter, the following plan is a simple step-by-step example of how a DBA would go about answering the first question in this chapter, "How much storage will the SQL Server need six months from now?"

The amount of storage needed for a SQL Server is dependent upon the size of the databases housed on that server. In the following example, database size will be the metric of focus that will be collected and analyzed.

Step 1: The Repository

For this example, the repository will simply be a new database on an existing SQL Server. Concern will not be placed on trying to create an enterprise-wide repository supporting every SQL Server in the company. That kind of infrastructure is very organization-specific, so rather than create an example that does not fit, a basic example will be created that can be extended as needed.

The first step is to decide on a database name and create a new database on the SQL Server. In a burst of creativity, this database will be named, REPOSITORY.

Next, create a table in the REPOSITORY database to store storage-usage statistics for the databases on the SQL Server. Name this table, *space_hist_db*, to reflect the fact that historical space statistics are being collected on these databases:

```
CREATE TABLE dbo.space_hist_db
(
    StatDate       smalldatetime NULL,
    DBName         varchar(128)  NULL,
    AllocatedMB    int           NULL,
    ReservedMB     int           NULL,
    UsedMB         int           NULL,
    DataMB         int           NULL,
    IndexMB        int           NULL,
    UnusedMB       int           NULL,
    UnreservedMB   int           NULL
)
```

Step 2: Collecting Statistics

Now that there is a historical table in the repository database, it needs to be populated. To do so, the following *sp_perf_space_db* procedure can be used:

🖫 sp_perf_space_db
```
-- Script is available in the Online Code Depot
```

There are a few things to note about this procedure. First, it has been created in the master database and spelled with the "*sp_*" prefix. This stands for "special procedure" or more often called, "system procedure". The reason these procedures are special is that although they reside in the master database, they can be executed from any database.

This feature is what allows the DBA to execute procedures such as the *sp_dboption* procedure from any database. Rather than deploying the same code to every application database, Microsoft has wisely collected all

---

such procedures in the master database and provided the means to access them from anywhere.

This feature has been used to make the space statistics collection easier. The *sp_perf_space_db* procedure will gather space statistics for the database from which the procedure is executed.

The wisdom for creating procedures in the master database may be debated. Microsoft will discourage it. However, Microsoft even discourages the querying of the *sys%* tables in favor of the *information_schema* views. Most DBAs still look at the *sys%* tables; however, DBAs are more accustomed to making rules rather than following them.

The *sp_perf_space_db* procedure is only one example of many different approaches that can be utilized in the collection of database space statistics. This example captures *dbcc showfilestats* as well as summarizing space metrics from the *sysindexes* table.

Step 3: Scheduling Statistical Collections

The next step is the scheduling of the execution of the *sp_perf_space_db* procedure for each database on the server.

One way to execute this procedure for each database is by use of the *sp_MSforeachdb* procedure. Another is with equivalent code such as the following:

```
DECLARE @name varchar(128),
        @sqlstr varchar(80)

DECLARE database_cursor CURSOR
    FOR SELECT name
            FROM master..sysdatabases

OPEN database_cursor

FETCH NEXT FROM database_cursor
        INTO @name

WHILE (@@fetch_status = 0)
  BEGIN
```

```
    SELECT @sqlstr = 'EXEC '+@name+'..sp_perf_space_db '
    EXEC(@sqlstr)
    FETCH NEXT FROM database_cursor INTO @name
  END

CLOSE database_cursor

DEALLOCATE database_cursor
go
```

The SQL Server Agent can then be used to schedule the code for periodic execution. The schedule frequency will be dependent on the volatility of the databases on the SQL Server. A weekly schedule is a good starting point. Though, on very slow-growth database servers, scheduling space collection on a monthly basis is also acceptable.

Step 4: Setting up Trend Analysis

Finally, the good stuff! After some time has passed, there will be historical space statistics in the *space_hist_db* table of the REPOSITORY database. Now, the DBA is in a position to perform a linear regression analysis on the data. This is a fancy term with a simple meaning: how close does the data fit to a straight line?

For example, suppose for database XYZ, the UsedMB value in the *space_hist_db* started at 350 at week zero, increased to 370 the following week, 392 the next week, 411 the next and on the fourth week was at 429. The UsedMB value is growing by about 20MB per week. If these values are plotted on a chart and a line drawn through them, it would almost be a straight line. Or, if a straight line was drawn from week zero (350) to week four (429), it would be seen that the plotted points in between were all very close to the line.

Linear regression analysis is the act of mathematically drawing a straight line and making a judgment about how close the points are to that line.

It is worth noting a counter-example here. Suppose UsedMB was 350 at week zero, remained unchanged the next week, rose to 375 the next, increased to 500 the next, and then remained unchanged again on week four. Can a straight line approximate this data growth? No, not very well. This is a classical stair-step growth pattern in which an event is occurring on intra-week intervals causing the database to grow in spurts. Perhaps looking at space usage on a monthly basis will help even out the growth pattern.

In order to perform a trend analysis on the historical data, two things are needed: a procedure to perform the analysis and a table in which to store the analysis. So in the REPOSITORY database, the *linear_regression* table is created:

```
CREATE TABLE dbo.linear_regression
(
    X          float      NOT NULL,
    Y          float      NOT NULL,
    XY         float      NULL,
    X2         float      NULL,
    Y2         float      NULL,
    dataflag char(1)      NULL
)
go
```

Also in the repository database, the *proc_linear_regression* procedure is created:

💾 proc_linear_regression

```
-- Script is available in the Online Code Depot
```

The final piece of this puzzle is to insert the historical space data into the *linear_regression* table:

```
insert into linear_regression (X,Y)
select
CONVERT(int,DATEPART(yy,StatDate))+
      CONVERT(int,DATEPART(dy,StatDate))/366.0,
      SUM(UsedMB)
  from
space_hist_db
 group by
      CONVERT(int,DATEPART(yy,StatDate))+
      CONVERT(int,DATEPART(dy,StatDate))/366.0
 order by
1
```

What is happening here is that two data elements are being pulled from the historical space table and are being plugged into the *linear_regression* table as "X,Y" coordinates.

The X value will always be the date element. In order to perform arithmetic on it, the date is converted into a decimal approximation. This is accomplished simply by dividing the day number by 366.0 to get a decimal fraction and adding that fraction to the year. For example, July 1, 2005 would be represented by an X value of about 2005.5.

The Y value is always the element being measured; in this case the sum of the UsedMB for all the databases at each collection time.

Now, all that is left to do is to execute the *proc_linear_regression* procedure and then review the output. The output will look something like the following:

```
Data values used for analysis:

  X                            Y
-------------------------    -----------------------------
2004.669398                  10.0
2004.751366                  15.0
2004.836065                  21.0
2004.918032                  27.0
2005.0027319999999           34.0
2005.0874309999999           40.0

Estimated regression equation: Y = -145932 + 72.8009*X

Rate of change (daily): 0.199402
Rate of change (weekly): 1.39618
Rate of change (monthly): 5.98358
Rate of change (yearly): 72.8009

Coefficient of determination: 0.998223 (the closer to 1.0 the better)
```

The beginning of the output simply displays the data used for the analysis. Check it to ensure it matches with the one being analyzed.

The next line is the mathematical equation that best describes the data. It is also the information used for the forecasting to be performed next, although another procedure will do that work for the DBA. Mostly this output is there for show. If the DBA is creating a case to present to management for a new server based on database growth, this equation and some estimated cost numbers can be thrown at them. Seeing these numbers will often scare them into giving in to the DBA's demands.

The next bit of output is the rate of change values. These can be valuable because they are something everyone can understand. In the example above, the databases on the server are growing at an annual rate of about 73MB. Not a very impressive example, yet it has been noted in other circumstances, growth rates of 300GB/year. That is usually enough to get a project underway to do some data purging.

The final, and most important, line of output is the "coefficient of determination." This value presents a gauge of how well the data fits into a straight line. A value of one is the maximum. This means that every point of data falls exactly on the straight line between the first X value and the last. Most often a value of something greater than 0.90 will be seen. If this value is much lower than 0.90, this should be viewed as a warning to not place much confidence in the linear regression (e.g. it does not fit a straight line very well). For example, if the result is a coefficient of determination below 0.80, this analysis should be completely forgotten and another value or timeframe should be sought for the analysis.

Step 5: Predicting the Future

And now the final piece of the puzzle; predicting the future. Assuming there is a good linear regression analysis with a coefficient of determination fairly close to 1.0, this straight line is ready to extend on the imaginary graph into the future.

To accomplish this, the DBA will need one more stored procedure: the *proc_linear_regression_forecast* procedure.

proc_linear_regression_forecast
-- Script is available in the Online Code Depot

To run this query, the DBA will need to pick sample X values to pass into the procedure. As stated before, these are dates and since arithmetic is performed on them, the dates will need to be converted to a decimal approximation.

In this example, dates are chosen that represent the quarters of the year. Thus April 1, 2005 is about 2005.25, July 1, 2005 about 2005.50, October 1, 2005 about 2005.75 and January 1, 2006 is about 2006.00. Given these values, the *proc_linear_regression_forecast* procedure is executed four times like the following:

```
exec proc_linear_regression_forecast 2005.25
exec proc_linear_regression_forecast 2005.50
exec proc_linear_regression_forecast 2005.75
exec proc_linear_regression_forecast 2006.00
```

The output is simply one line for each execution such as the following:

```
Forecasted value of Y when X=2005.25 is 51.6181
Forecasted value of Y when X=2005.5 is 69.8183
Forecasted value of Y when X=2005.75 is 88.0185
Forecasted value of Y when X=2006 is 106.219
```

This reveals that by 2006 the databases on this server will be using 106MB of space. Although the output is quite specific (i.e. 106.219), it is meant to be an approximation, not an exact value. The figure is rounded in whichever direction serves the DBA's agenda the best!

Conclusion

It is tough for a busy DBA charged with several SQL Servers to be proactive instead of constantly being engaged in firefighting. However, capacity planning is one practice that pays huge dividends toward getting there. The biggest issue is not: should capacity planning be utilized? It is: how one will go about it? Whether deciding to build an individual capacity planning system or to buy a third party solution, the information in this chapter can be used to ensure the DBA stays on the right track.

The next chapter will explain how to use all the information gained, from the various performance analysis methods and capacity planning studies, to make smart tuning decisions.

Performance Lifecycle Management: Step 5

Tuning that Makes a Difference

It is more important than ever before that the database administrator's time is not wasted. The explosions in database growth and sheer numbers of managed databases coupled with increased responsibilities signify that every minute of every day is nearly always spoken for. Polls taken of DBAs consistently show the number one task, both in terms of importance and time spent, is monitoring and tuning databases for better performance. Even in an age of supposedly self-managing database engines, it appears DBAs will always have their hands full in this area.

This being the case, it is critical for the DBA to know how to approach tuning in a way such that efforts are rewarded with substantial performance improvements. Many DBAs spend hours tweaking areas of the system that end up not having any serious impact in the overall efficiency of SQL Server. With an increasing workload, this is the last thing they want to focus energy on.

The use of a tuning roadmap that works efficiently and can be systematically followed and applied to all SQL Servers is highly desirable. Finding the needles in the SQL Server haystack is the first step in improving overall efficiency. By smartly following the performance diagnostic methods of bottleneck, workload, and ratio analysis, pinpointing the various areas of SQL Server that need optimization should not be a problem.

What happens once the issues have been identified? Successful DBAs must always be able to correlate their diagnostics with proven resolutions so performance stays razor sharp. While performance tuning will always be an individualized process and somewhat of an art, there is a broad, three step roadmap available to the DBA to be used to work through to keep SQL Server running well.

The Simplified Performance Tuning Model

When approaching tuning in SQL Server, the DBA will work through the following three areas:

- Configuration

- SQL Optimization

- Physical Design Revisions

That's it. There can be a lot of complexity and effort involved in working through these steps, but broadly speaking, these are the categories the DBA will be engaged in.

The first thing to understand is these three areas are presented in reverse order of their usual performance impact. This means making configuration changes will buy the least amount of performance optimization. Making SQL optimization changes will buy more performance optimization, and making physical design revisions has the largest potential for performance increase.

These steps are presented according to ease of application. It is not usually a problem to make SQL Server parameterization or server configuration tweaks. SQL optimization is less dangerous and less complex than making physical design revisions.

The remaining sections of this chapter will work through each step and correlate diagnostics presented in earlier chapters with recommendations for performance improvement. The meaning of the various diagnostics along with how to obtain them will not be covered again. Therefore, if a particular statistic is needed, the index of this book should be utilized to locate the correct chapter in which the particular metric is covered in detail.

Making Configuration Changes

Some database engines, such as Oracle, have renowned reputations for being complex to tune from a configuration standpoint. In an effort to overcome this reputation, Oracle has worked diligently with each new release to reduce the number of configuration parameters required to manage their engine, so much so that Oracle10g comes close to looking like SQL Server in some respects.

By contrast, SQL Server has never had many configuration parameters to deal with and has offered automatic management of the most commonly tweaked areas such as memory. This does not mean that the DBA's input is not necessary. To the contrary, from time to time manual configuration will be required. With that in mind, the following sections will examine some of the more common areas which the DBA might have to manually manipulate.

When to Consider More Memory

The most common set of configuration parameters that DBAs have had to manage are those related to memory. However, starting with version 7.0, Microsoft has provided auto-management for both the total amount of server RAM given to SQL Server as well as the allocation of the different memory regions such as the buffer and plan cache.

The *min server memory* and *max server memory* parameters govern the total gift of RAM provided SQL Server from the Windows machine. These two parameters default in such a way as to allow SQL Server to dynamically adjust the feed of memory to the database engine. In normal circumstances, there is little need to disengage from SQL Server autopilot and take manual control of memory allocations. It is not uncommon for SQL Server to experience memory pressure and require more memory than it is possible for it to obtain at that time.

When deciding whether SQL Server could benefit from more physical memory, the following checklist can be used:

- Is the SQL Server total server memory statistic at or near the target memory measure? If so, SQL Server may need more RAM but be physically constrained from allocating more.

- Is the SQL Server page life expectancy statistic less than 300? If TRUE, and large table scans do not seem to be a problem, a shortage of RAM may be the cause.

- Are the key memory ratios: buffer cache; plan cache; and ad-hoc SQL below desired levels? While not the best indicators of memory pressure, they can indicate a memory constrained server.

- Is the Windows performance counter of Memory: Available Bytes consistently low or near zero?

- Is the Windows performance counter of Memory: Pages/sec consistently high, indicating paging and swapping activity?

Another situation in which more memory may be needed occurs when numerous query plans are involved in hash joins or sort operations. These particular actions require more memory resources than other query-based operations and may benefit from increasing the *min memory per query* parameter. Increasing the default may increase performance for these types of SQL requests, but they will also increase overall memory consumption.

More memory may not be the silver bullet for an ailing SQL Server, but it can work miracles in the right situation in which a server has been accidently undersized for the workload.

Avoiding Maximum Limit Problems

Previous chapters in this book addressed the situation of avoiding immediate bottlenecks; problems that bring events to an abrupt halt. This type of bottleneck can occur because certain configuration limits are set too low. Earlier versions of SQL Server suffered from this problem, but Microsoft now auto-manages the two most common parameters that used to cause problems: *open objects* and *locks*.

Although this situation should not be a problem any longer, if the SQL Server error log is reporting errors based on the above configuration parameters, someone may have altered the settings from the default, auto-managed state.

Other Parameters that Deserve a Look

There are only a few more configuration parameters that may need tweaking from time to time; the *network packet size* parameter; the *fill factor* configuration parameter; and the *priority boost* parameter.

The *network packet size* parameter controls the size of the fixed chunks of data that are sent back and forth between clients and SQL Server. If there is an application that routinely bulk loads lots of data into a database or transfers large volumes of text or image data, this parameter can be increased from its default of four KB. Another performance indicator is increased wait count and wait time activity in the NETWORKIO wait event of SQL Server. Increasing the parameter to eight KB or more can result in fewer network reads and writes.

The *fill factor* configuration parameter globally controls the *fillfactor* amount used for index creation operations that do not specify the *fillfactor* option. An upcoming section will deal more thoroughly with

---

fillfactor, but for now, if the DBA knows that there are SQL Server-driven applications that are very INSERT and UPDATE intensive, this option can be changed to something other than the default. This normally involves changing *fillfactor* to a figure in the neighborhood of 50-70%.

Finally, if the Windows server is a dedicated SQL Server machine, the *priority boost* parameter can be set to a value of one. This indicates that SQL Server should run at a higher priority than other processes on the Windows machine. Microsoft only recommends doing this on multi-CPU boxes that are dedicated to running SQL Server.

Miscellaneous Hardware Configuration Notes

DBAs are now finding their voices heard during server purchasing decisions since they know all too well that the wrong hardware can cripple database systems from the start. In the database world, there are a variety of opinions on things to look for and watch out for regarding server purchasing decisions. The following list highlights a few of the most common points:

- The drive speed does make a difference. 15K RPM is significantly faster than 10K.

- The array controller is the most important piece of hardware on a database server assuming no SAN attached. If well tuned, database servers always end up being I/O constrained. The array controller will be the deciding factor on I/O throughput.

- It is OK to turn write-caching ON in the array controller. In fact, it is necessary for top performance.

- Even if the database is on a SAN, experience has taught many DBAs that it is best to still get a good array controller and use it for local drives housing the transaction log volume; usually a mirrored pair.

- Even with the best array controller and write-caching turned ON, RAID-5 is still a performance loser. RAID1+0 or equivalent is by far the best for both performance and availability.

- CPU speed is important, but the GHz rating is not the most important factor. Actual throughput is better on chips with more on-board cache, to the point that a slower clock-speed chip may out-perform a higher speed chip. Price can sometimes be used as a guideline for how good (fast) a chip is. The cheap stuff should be avoided.

Honest Talk about Optimizing SQL

Most likely, DBAs have a handful of authors they read and reference regularly because those authors have found a way to communicate information to them in a clear and concise manner. In the Oracle world, Tom Kyte, is one such author. Tom's practical present-and-prove-it approach is difficult to beat and is never laced with mythological sayings that have no basis of fact in the real world. Many flock to his, "Ask Tom" website where he answers questions from Oracle users around the world.

The following section includes one such Q & A concerning tuning SQL. Even though this book is dealing with SQL Server, this question and answer is still very applicable.

From Kyte's website:

You Asked:

I am new in tuning sql statements. Can u give a methodology of tuning the SQL statements?

and we said...

Here is a short extract from a book I am working on. The short answer is if you want a 10 step guide to tuning a query, buy a piece of software. You are not needed in this process, anyone can put a query in, get a query out and run it to see if it is faster. There are tons of these tools on the market. They work using rules (heuristics) and can tune maybe 1% of the problem queries out there. They APPEAR to be able to tune a much larger percent but that is only because the people using these tools never look at the outcome -- hence they continue to make the same basic mistakes over and over and over.

If you want to really be able to tune the other 99% of the queries out there, knowledge of lots of stuff -- physical storage mechanisms, access paths, how the optimizer works - thats the only way.

This answer is so right on! It is a great answer because Kyte is a VP of Oracle, an expert at tuning SQL code, and knows that his company sells tools that supposedly automatically tune SQL for their customers. His advice rings true in the SQL Server world as well. Although a lot of SQL Server code has been rewritten and optimized, a guaranteed set of rules that will work in every situation does not exist. Before reading the rest of this section, it is important the DBA understands that optimizing SQL code will always be an individualized process challenging even the best DBA.

Although there is no guaranteed set of rules, there is a set of guiding principles that can be used in SQL optimizing exercises. If it appears challenging on this level, imagine writing internal SQL and procedures for 70,000+ customers who are hard core database professionals that have little pity for software that does not run as fast as they want! A little experience can go a long way in solving big problems.

The SQL optimization roadmap of guiding principles is as follows:

- Ready the SQL optimization toolbox.
- Validate the SQL.

- Obtain code performance baseline.

- EXPLAIN to get access path information.

- Update and understand key object statistics.

- Look for object based solutions.

- Rewrite code and perform new benchmarks.

- Perform statistical comparison and select best case.

The SQL Optimization Toolbox

To troubleshoot and optimize SQL and stored procedures, software is needed that helps the DBA quickly diagnose a particular query, understand what the optimizer is doing, get basic performance and execution statistics, and easily test different rewrite combinations. Software exists that does more than this, but most optimization pro's get the majority of their work accomplished with these basic features.

Fortunately, everything described above can be found in Microsoft's Query Analyzer tool, which has been bundled into SQL Server 2005's Management Studio. Although many SQL Server professionals use Query Analyzer to run queries, some do not exploit the various built in functions of the tool.

Although looking at EXPLAIN plans is important, the ability to see the performance execution metrics at the start of, and during optimization sessions is the most valuable aid in troubleshooting. The trace capability is especially useful when tuning procedures as the lines of code can be pinpointed that are consuming the most I/O, CPU, etc. Query Analyzer makes it easy to trace and obtain all statistics necessary when tuning a piece of SQL code.

Most SQL Server folks rarely use the trace or execution statistics capability of Query Analyzer. These are powerful tools and should be utilized during a tuning session. Figure 10.1 is a representation of the results of using the SQL trace capability in Query Analyzer to view Procedure Execution Statistics.

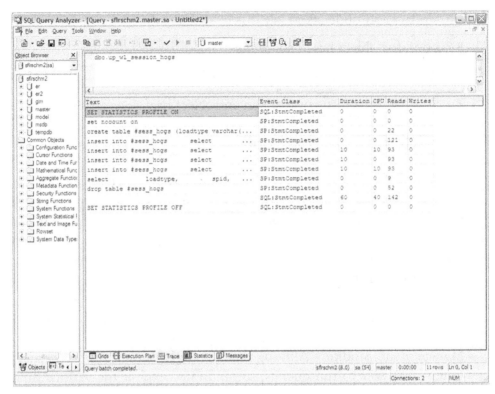

Figure 10.1: *Using the SQL trace capability in Query Analyzer to view Procedure Execution Statistics.*

Validate the SQL

Validating SQL seems rather straightforward, but developers often write or paste SQL into an application without first seeing if it is actually syntactically correct. Web developers are the worst offenders because many of the tools they employ do not provide a parser to check SQL code. Consequently, they often code or paste some SQL into their controls and hope for the best. Obviously, this is not the best way to work. Syntax problems will reappear continuously and productivity will begin a downward slide.

Ideally, DBAs and developers should do their work in an integrated development environment that offers the ability to quickly check the validity. In other words, they should be able to parse SQL code. Parsing validates security access to the underlying objects, ensures object definition names or references are correct and in order, and confirms the underlying syntax is valid and free of errors.

Obtain a Baseline

Before commencing any optimization attempts, the DBA should obtain a performance baseline that provides the execution metrics of the query or stored code. At a minimum, elapsed execution time, CPU utilization, and I/O resource usage should be understood.

The DBA may already have such metrics if SQL was identified from trace activities, but if not, these statistics are easy to get. All one is required to do is to turn on the SHOW SERVER TRACE and SHOW CLIENT STATISTICS options of Query Analyzer, run the code, and SQL Server will then give the baseline needed.

Another piece of information important to have, yet often ignored, concerns the number of times SQL or stored code is run on a daily basis. Knowing this information is critical for a couple of reasons.

First, the DBA should not waste valuable time tuning SQL that is seldom run on the server because it is likely to have little impact on overall performance levels.

Next, the DBA should not be fooled by something that appears to run quickly and is run a lot. Taking a query down from two seconds to one will have quite an impact if the SQL is run thousands of times per day on SQL Server.

Unfortunately, this piece of information is not easy to obtain in SQL Server 7 – 2000 even with SQL Profiler or tracing. In SQL Server 2005, however, a new dynamic management view has been introduced that does track the execution count of routinely executed SQL. If one is currently using SQL Server 2005, the *sql_stats_2005* query below can be used to get execution metrics as well as other useful information:

📄 **sql_stats_2005.sql**

```
-- Script is available in the Online Code Depot
```

EXPLAIN and Understand

The next stop is to review an EXPLAIN plan for the query or stored code. SQL Server makes it exceptionally easy to obtain EXPLAIN plans. Query Analyzer has an excellent visual EXPLAIN plan that tops anything offered by Microsoft's database competitors. Other query tools can make use of the set *showplan_all on* option to obtain an EXPLAIN of the code that is being run.

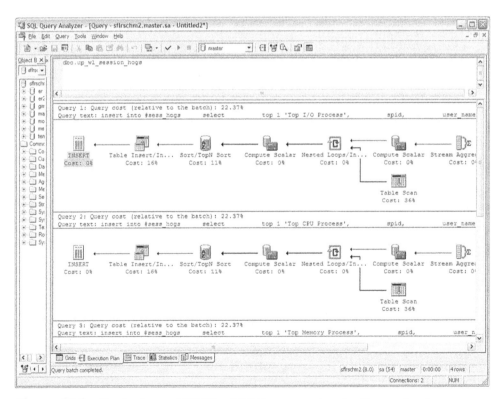

Figure 10.2: *Reviewing an EXPLAIN for a procedure in Query Analyzer.*

EXPLAIN plans are read from top to bottom and right to left. Without a doubt, some EXPLAIN plans can get very unwieldy to deal with so the DBA should have in place a method for cherry-picking areas of an EXPLAIN on which to focus. A good general list of top offenders to work from is noted as follows:

- Operations with excessive cost.

- Nasty join operations.

- Table and index scans.

- Large result sets.

- Unnecessary sorts.

- Object warnings.

Excessive Cost

Query analyzer has a nice feature in that it presents the cost of each step as a percentage, so the DBA can quickly tell what areas of a query appear to be the resource hogs.

Because there are exceptions to every rule, there will be times when the highest cost operations are not the culprits in reducing a query's performance; however, it is a good place to start.

Nasty Join Operations

There are several join operations that should be avoided in a query. Leading the pack is the Cartesian join. It normally appears only as a coding mistake on the part of the user who issued the query. A Cartesian join means there are two tables involved in a query that have not been properly joined together through some relational column pairing. For example:

```
select
    patient_id
from
    admission a,
    patient b
where
    patient_last_name like 'JUNG%'
```

The two tables in the above query have not been paired together through a common relational column that is present in both tables; therefore, SQL Server will have to utilize a Cartesian join. The Cartesian join multiplies the number of rows in the first table by the number of rows in the second table to arrive at the result set.

To guard against Cartesian joins, the standard rule of thumb is there must be (N − 1) number of join predicates, where N represents the number of tables in the FROM clause. A Cartesian product can be spotted easily in the EXPLAIN as there will be a larger signaled result set than expected.

Besides Cartesian joins, be on the lookout for other join operations that can contribute to excessive run times. The most common heavy-duty joins are hash and merge joins. These joins perform more in-memory processing than nested loop joins, and therefore, the DBA will see higher CPU and memory usage from these operations.

Often, indexing changes can transform the hash join into a nested loop join. Since each situation is different, keep a close eye on the performance execution metrics as different combinations are tried.

Table and Index Scans

When are scans good? If the objects are small in physical size, it is usually more efficient for SQL Server to cache the object and scan it rather than utilizing an indexing strategy. If a query needs to return all the rows in a particular table and a covering index does not exist, a scan is the only door left open to SQL Server.

However, large table scans should be avoided as they take serious resources to perform and often flood the buffer cache with data pages that are not likely to be re-read. Indexing is usually the remedy for such situations; however, it must be ensured that the actual WHERE clause is not written in a way that negates the use of an index.

If an indexing strategy will not work and only a subset of a table's data is needed, the DBA can investigate the use of partitioning to cut down on scan times. In SQL Server 7 and 2000, tables can be manually partitioned through a technique called horizontal partitioning, but with SQL Server 2005, full object partitioning is supported through DDL. Horizontal partitioning will be covered later in an upcoming section.

In any event, the savvy DBA should be on the lookout for SCAN operations that show up in the EXPLAIN plans versus SEEKs. SEEKs attempt to go directly to the rows necessary to fulfill a request; whereas scans read the whole object.

Finally, using some functions and expressions in WHERE predicates can totally negate the use of indexes that could otherwise be used by the optimizer. An example of a suppression WHERE predicate would be as follows:

```
select
    count(*)
from
    patient
where
    substring(patient_name,1,5) = 'JOHNS'
```

To utilize an index, the query could be rewritten in the following fashion:

```
select
    count(*)
from
    patient
where
    patient_name like 'JOHNS%'
```

Large Result Sets

Unnecessary I/O is something to avoid, so in the EXPLAIN, look for result sets that appear to return excessive numbers of rows. In this instance, the rows are not required for query satisfaction.

One sure ticket to excessive row returns is to mistakenly code a Cartesian product.

Unnecessary Sorts

Is the ORDER BY clause really necessary? Memory sorts are usually fine, but when sorts go to disk and *tempdb*, this is where the query can hit the skids. This is especially true if the *tempdb* is sitting on a RAID5 physical device.

The DBA should be on the lookout for operations that force a sort without knowledge, such as a query that uses DISTINCT to eliminate duplicate rows or a UNION operator.

Object Warnings

The SQL Server optimizer does its best when deciding upon the access path to take for query satisfaction. However, the DBA can help the optimizer by ensuring that it has current statistics to work with. The Query Analyzer EXPLAIN plan will provide warnings when various object statistics are missing as does the text-based EXPLAIN plans run through other SQL editors.

By setting the database options of *auto create statistics* and *auto update statistics*, SQL Server will try to keep object statistics up to date. As an alternative, the UPDATE STATISTICS command can be run on objects in either ad-hoc fashion or through a job that periodically updates the data dictionary.

Update and Review Object Statistics

When writing efficient SQL, it is imperative to know the demographics and shape of the objects that code will bump up against. For most databases, all the information ever needed, can be found in the data dictionary, but when querying the dictionary for object statistics, make sure accurate information is being viewed.

Methods for keeping object statistics up to date by setting the *auto create statistics* and *auto update statistics* options of a particular database have already been covered. In addition, the UPDATE STATISTICS command can be used. Many DBAs have reported that Microsoft's automatic updates do not supply as high quality a job as the manual UPDATE STATISTICS command. To be safe, it wise to schedule off-hours updates of important objects.

Whatever path is chosen to update objects, the DBA should make a practice of keeping data in the dictionary current, especially for databases that are dynamic in nature. Scheduling object updates in a nightly maintenance plan for dynamic databases is a wise decision as fresh statistics help the optimizer make more informed choices on which path to follow when routing queries to the requested data.

Now, the DBA knows to keep object statistics up to date. When tuning SQL, what types of metrics should the DBA look for in objects to help make intelligent coding choices? Although this list is certainly not exhaustive, for tables, the DBA should start by reviewing the following items:

- Row Counts: No heavy explanation is needed for why one should look at this statistic. Avoid full scans on beefy tables with large row counts. Proper index placement becomes quite important on such tables. Other reasons for reviewing row counts include physical redesign decisions. Perhaps a table has grown larger than anticipated and is now eligible for partitioning? Scanning a single partition in a table is a lot less work than running through the entire table.

- Forwarded Row Counts: Row forwarding can be a thorn in the side of an otherwise well written SQL statement. Forwarded records can reduce performance because additional I/O is involved in first obtainin the record pointer to the relocated row and then the row itself. More information about finding and diagnosing the severity of table issues has been included in Chapter 5.

- Extent Proximity: SQL Server has a prefetch mechanism called the Read Ahead manager that pulls data it believes will be needed for operations, such as full table scans, into the memory caches. Having the data already present in memory ensures that response times are the shortest possible. However, the Read Ahead manager's ability to perform as efficiently as possible is somewhat dependent on the organization of the data that it prefetches. If the data is contiguous in nature, the Read Ahead manager can work very well and read large chunks of data at a time. However, if the data is scattered and mixed throughout extents that contain other objects, the Read Ahead manager cannot move in one fluid direction and instead must skip around the file(s) to obtain the data it believes will be needed. Again, Chapter 5 contains material regarding the shaping of objects with respect to extent proximity.

- Miscellaneous Properties: There are several other performance boosting properties the DBA may want to set for tables. For example, small lookup tables may benefit from being pinned in memory to keep their pages available in the buffer cache.

Indexes have their own unique set of items that need to be reviewed occasionally. Some of these include the following:

- Selectivity/Unique Keys: Indexes by nature normally work best when selectivity is high. In other words, the numbers of unique values are many. The exception to this rule is the bitmap index, which does not exist for SQL Server. The selectivity of indexes should be periodically examined to see if indexes that use to contain many unique values are now ones that are losing their uniqueness rank. This can be accomplished via the DBCC SHOW_STATISTICS command.

- Depth: The tree depth of an index will reveal if the index has undergone numerous splits and other destructive activity. Typically, indexes with tree depths greater than three or four are good candidates for rebuilds, an activity that hopefully will improve access speed. This data can be acquired via the fragmentation procedures presented in Chapter 5.

Look for Object-Based Solutions

Reworking join predicates and using subqueries instead of joins can produce dramatic differences in query response time. However, the technique required to help a slow running piece of SQL often includes adding or altering something at the physical design level. An upcoming section of this chapter will deal with this topic in more detail. For now, just know that one should always be thinking about what can be done at database level to enhance query speed. For example:

- Adding new indexes to eliminate scan operations.

- Altering existing indexes to create covering indexes or increase the effectiveness of composite indexes.

- Altering the clustered index choice for a particular table.

- Removing indexes for tables that are the targets of heavy BCP or INSERT, UPDATE and DELETE operations. Indexes may be added once data modification tasks have finished.

- Denormalizing an excessively normalized database to decrease join operations.

- Building a reporting sub-structure that can support resource intensive SELECT queries.

- Partitioning data to reduce table width or data volumes. This must be manually performed in SQL Server 7 – 2000, but can be done through DDL in SQL Server 2005.

- Pinning small lookup tables in memory to speed access to data that is often referenced.

- Investigating the use of data archive software that archives older, seldom used data onto other servers, which can still be accessed if need be, and leaves often referenced data on the primary server.

- Putting a plan in place to automatically eliminate fragmentation in indexes and tables that are subject to actions that frequently disorganize them.

Rewrite and Benchmark

When the SQL is valid, the objects are in order, and object-based resolutions have been investigated, it is time to begin trying different code combinations in hopes of improving the query's performance. This is where SQL tuning becomes an art.

Using hints, changing subqueries to joins, switching UNION's to UNION ALL's can become time consuming but rewarding as tuning becomes easier.

Once the DBA has assembled a suite of new SQL combinations for the existing query, it is time to actually send them through the database to see if anything is being accomplished. When performing these informal benchmarks, it is important to do them correctly.

For example, each query should not just be executed one time and the measurements recorded. First time executions typically take longer than subsequent tries due to parse activity and data being read in the first time from disk. At a minimum, each new query should be sent through three to four times with the high and low readings thrown out.

Statistically Compare Cases and Select a Winner

Usually, all that is needed to determine a winning rewrite is to examine execution time or duration in a trace. Sometimes it is not so clear, so other factors may come into play such as CPU or I/O utilization. Most of the time, there will be one that stands out screaming, "Pick me!"

When to Revisit

The DBA may think the job is over once optimized SQL code has been delivered into production. In some shops, this thought may be right. One should not be surprised, however, if the once well-running SQL is returned with the mandate to fix it again. Why might this happen? It is not uncommon for fast code to become sluggish in the following circumstances:

- Data Volume Changes: Code that once ran well with objects having small data volumes may turn into something that crawls along when those same objects are a little heftier in size.

- Missing Indexes: Occasionally, another DBA may remove an index on a table that is causing slowdowns during INSERT, UPDATE, and DELETE operations. Unfortunately, that index may have been critical to the success of a particular query and a compromise may have to be reached with the DBA about what to do.

There are plenty of other circumstances that can take the life out of what once was a good SQL query. The DBA should always be ready to step back through a checklist and see what new miracle can be delivered.

Physical Design Revisions

As has been repeated throughout this book, the biggest area for performance gains almost always comes from things done at the physical design level. Of course, it is always best if a DBA creates a proper physical design in the first place, so one should strive to create a physical design that excels from the start.

Even the best designs need tweaking from time to time, so the DBA can expect to revise certain areas of the design to keep performance high. These areas include the following:

- Indexing
- File and Object Placements

- Partitioning

- General Denormalization

Some of these areas may be difficult to accomplish if dealing with packaged applications, but there are areas in which the DBA still has some degree of control. Before each of these points is explained in detail, it is advantageous to know what tools Microsoft provides to help with these tasks.

Using Microsoft Supplied Aids

There are two main weapons that Microsoft supplies to help with deciding what to change at the physical design level. These weapons are as follows:

- Index or Database Tuning Wizard

- Best Practices Analyzer

The Index Tuning Wizard has been around for a quite some time. The Best Practices Analyzer has only recently been introduced to help enforce various physical design rules, as well as other common practices.

Index/Database Tuning Wizard

The Index Tuning Wizard has its critics, yet it has its champions as well. The concept is excellent: give SQL Server an SQL-based workload or set of individual queries to work with, and let the SQL Server reveal what object-based solutions may be of benefit in improving performance.

 Critics say the Index Tuning Wizard fails on many occasions to recommend a proper indexing scheme or suggests indexes that are ineffective. However, as has already been mentioned, tuning SQL and a database's physical design is an art form. Thus, it is never a bad idea to get advice from as many sources as possible. Besides, just like anything else, the Index Tuning Wizard has gotten better over time, so it is worth a try.

In SQL Server 2005, the utility has been renamed the Database Tuning Advisor and has been updated to include partitioning recommendations. Figure 10.3 is a representation of the SQL Server 2005 Database Tuning Advisor.

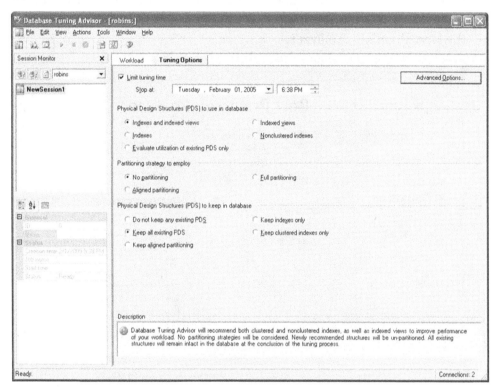

Figure 10.3: *The SQL Server 2005 Database Tuning Advisor.*

The DBA can feed either utility a trace file created through server-side tracing or SQL Profiler or a list of queries for SQL Server to examine. Thus, the tool performs a thorough examination of the database and SQL structures and presents recommendations.

Again, the Index/Database Tuning Wizard/Advisor is not perfect, but can prove helpful in the right situations.

Best Practices Analyzer

A product not bundled with SQL Server is the Best Practices Analyzer, which was released to help DBAs enforce standards on their managed SQL Servers. A DBA can choose the servers to interrogate and then choose what they would like to check from a pre-defined list of rules. Figure 10.4 is a representation of how enforcement rules are defined in the Best Practices Analyzer.

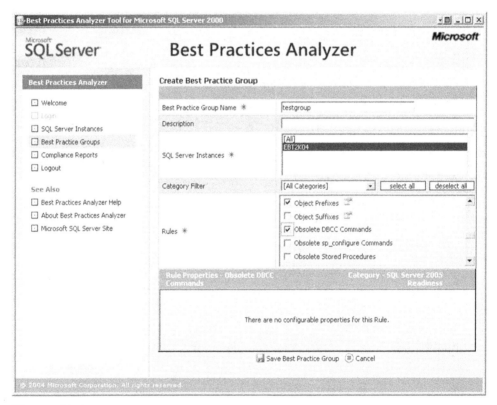

Figure 10.4: *Defining enforcement rules in the Best Practices Analyzer.*

While it is nice to have such a tool to work on SQL Servers, as of this writing, there are some drawbacks to the product. Some of the drawbacks are: not being able to define custom rules; and not being able to schedule periodic scans of SQL Servers. Microsoft is sure to enhance these areas in future releases.

Automating Physical Design Reviews

Knowing that practically every minute of time is often spoken for, it is important for the SQL Server DBA to automate as much work as possible. One automation scheme includes setting physical design reviews on autopilot and allowing Microsoft's supplied tools perform most of the work. The plan is as follows:

Step 1: Schedule the Collection of a Database Workload

A day of the week and timeframe should be chosen when activity for a particular database is representative of the normal workload. For example, one could choose every Wednesday between the hours of 1:00 p.m. and 4:00 p.m.

A stored procedure should be created or a standard T-SQL block of code used to start a server-side trace that catches the SQL workload, both ad-hoc SQL and stored code executions, for the time period. SQL Server traces make this easy as the DBA can pass in a parameter that automatically stops and closes the trace after a particular amount of time has elapsed.

For example, the following procedure, *up_weekly_workload,* deletes the trace file previously collected from the procedure and starts a new trace that automatically ends three hours from the time the trace begins.

🖫 up_weekly_workload
```
-- Script is available in the Online Code Depot
```

SQL Agent should be used to schedule the execution of the procedure at the start of the chosen day/time. The procedure will invoke and begin building a trace file that collects all the issued SQL statements. The *up_weekly_workload* procedure can be altered to focus on just a single database instead of an entire server, if desired.

Step 2: Feed the Trace Workload into the Index/Database Tuning Wizard

The second step is to schedule a job that invokes Microsoft's Index/Database Tuning Wizard from the command line by using the previously collected workload file as input.

Some DBAs do not know that the Index/Database Tuning Wizard can be invoked from the command line, but this can indeed be accomplished. For SQL Server 7 and 2000, the ITWIZ utility is the command line interface into the index tuning wizard. The syntax and arguments are as follows:

```
itwiz
    [-?] |
    [
        -D database_name {-i workload_file |
        -t workload_trace_table_name}
        -o script_file_name
        [-S server_name [\instance]]
        {
            {-U login_id [-P password]}
            | -E
        }
        [-f tuning_feature_set]
        [-K keep_existing_indexes]
        [-M recommendation_quality]
        [-B storage_bound]
        [-n number_of_queries]
        [-C max_columns_in_index]
        [-T table_list_file]
        [-m minimum_improvement]
        [-F] [-v]
    ]
```

Where:

- **-?**: Displays usage information.

- **-D** *database_name:* Specifies the name of the database to be tuned.

- **-i** *workload_file:* Specifies the name of the workload file to use as input for tuning. The file must be in one of these formats: .trc (SQL Profiler trace file); .sql (SQL file); or .log (SQL Server 7.0 trace file).

- **-t** *workload_table_name:* Specifies the name of a table containing the workload trace for tuning. The name is: [*server_name*].[*database_name*].[*owner_name*].*table_name*.

The first three parameters are optional and can be omitted by marking their positions with a period. Table 10.1 shows the default values for each.

PARAMETER	DEFAULT VALUE
server_name	server_name specified with –S option. If the –S option is not specified, server_name defaults to the local computer.
database_name	database_name specified with –D option.
owner_name	dbo.
table_name	None.

Table 10.1: *Default values for parameters.*

owner_name must be dbo. If any other value is specified, execution of ITWIZ will fail and an error will be returned.

- **-o** *script_file_name* :Specifies the name of the file to which ITWIZ writes the recommendation script. By default, output files are created in the current directory. The recommendation script contains the expected improvement if the recommendation is accepted.

- **-S** *server_name*[*instance*] :Specifies the computer and instance of SQL Server to connect to. If no *server_name* or *instance* is specified, ITWIZ connects to the default instance of SQL Server on the local computer. This option is required when executing ITWIZ from a remote computer on the network.

- **-U** *login_id* : Specifies the login ID used to connect to SQL Server.

- **-P** *password* : Specifies the password for the login ID. If this option is not used, ITWIZ prompts for a password. If this option is used without specifying a password, ITWIZ uses the default password of NULL.

- -E : Uses a trusted connection instead of requesting a password.

- -f *tuning_feature_set* : Specifies the features to be considered by ITWIZ for tuning.

VALUE	DESCRIPTION
0	All features (default)
1	Indexes only
2	Indexed views only. A (applies only to SQL Server 2000, Enterprise and Developer editions)

- -K *keep_existing_indexes* : Specifies whether ITWIZ is allowed to propose a recommendation that requires dropping one or more existing indexes.

VALUE	DESCRIPTION
0	Do not keep existing indexes
1	Keep all existing indexes (default)

- -M *recommendation_quality* : Specifies the desired point in the running time versus quality of recommendation tradeoff. Higher values of *recommendation_quality* yield better quality of recommendation. Currently, *recommendation_quality* can be one of the values shown in this table.

VALUE	DESCRIPTION
0	Fast mode
1	Medium mode (default)
2	Thorough analysis mode

Fast mode currently has the following restrictions:

- No new clustered indexes are recommended.

- No new indexed views are recommended.

- All existing indexes are kept. This is equivalent to specifying the **-K 1** option.

The combinations **-M 0 -K 0** and **-M 0 -f 2** are invalid and cannot be used. Also, when used in conjunction with **-M 0**, options **-f 0** and **–f 1** are equivalent.

- **-B** *storage_bound* : Specifies the maximum space, in megabytes, that can be consumed by the recommended index set. The default storage bound is three times the current data size or the maximum available space on all attached disk drives, or whichever is smaller. The current data size consists of all tables and clustered indexes.

- **-n** *number_of_queries* : Specifies the number of queries to be tuned. By default, 200 queries are randomly chosen from the specified workload file. If *number_of_queries* exceeds the number of queries in the workload file, all queries are tuned.

- **-C** *max_columns_in_index* : Specifies the maximum number of columns in indexes proposed by ITWIZ. The default value is 16. This is the maximum value allowed by SQL Server.

- **-T** *table_list_file* : Specifies the name of a file containing a list of tables to be tuned. Each table listed within the file should begin on a new line. Table names can be qualified by a user name, for example, DBO.AUTHORS. Optionally, to invoke the table-scaling feature, the name of a table can be followed by a number indicating the projected number of rows in the table.

The table-scaling feature enables studying recommended indexes on smaller scale sample databases. A reasonable size, several %, thousands of rows per table, should be used for the smaller sample database, otherwise the scaled data distribution histograms may be inaccurate and the set of recommended indexes for the sample database may be different from the index recommended for the full scale database.

This is the file format for *table_list_file*:

[owner.]table [number_of_rows]

[owner.]table [number_of_rows]

... ...

If the **-T** option is omitted, all user tables in the specified database are considered for tuning.

- **-m** *minimum_improvement* : If the **-m** option is specified, ITWIZ does not recommend any changes in the index configuration, unless the expected improvement in performance for the selected workload is at least *minimum_improvement%*. If all queries are not considered for tuning, see option **-n**, the queries not selected are not considered when the improvement is evaluated.

- **-F** : Permits ITWIZ to overwrite an existing output file. In the event that an output file with the same name already exists and **-F** is not specified, ITWIZ returns an error.

- **-v** : Enables verbose output from ITWIZ. If **-v** is not specified, ITWIZ directs only abbreviated information to the screen during execution.

For SQL Server 2005, the ITWIZ utility has been replaced by the *dta* executable. As of this writing, any new command line arguments have not been documented.

The DBA should, once again, use SQL Agent and schedule the running of the index/database tuning wizard with the trace file as input in off hours so as to not impact performance during prime working hours. The job type will be an operating system command style job and not a T-SQL based routine.

Unless there is a need to conserve resources on the machine as the analysis job runs, these guidelines should be followed when invoking either the index or database tuning wizard:

- Use zero, the default value, for the *tuning_feature_setting* parameter so all physical design options are considered.

- Use zero for the *keep_existing_indexes* option so SQL Server can recommend the removal of indexes that are not used.

- Use two for the *quality_of_recommendation* option so the most through analysis will be executed.

For example, a sample command line job that invokes the index tuning wizard, while accepting the defaults, for a server named *et2k08* and performs an analysis for a database called *big_database* and puts the recommendations in a file called *c:\script_trc.sql* would be:

```
itwiz -S et2k08 -U sa -P mypassword -D big_database -i
c:\big_database_query.trc -o c:\script_trc.sql -F
```

Intelligent Indexing

This book is not designed for those who are new to SQL Server, so the general indexing discussions that focus on what an index is, the types of indexes, etc. will be bypassed. Instead, this section will explain how best to index for performance. Keep in mind that each database's workload is different, but the following checklist can be utilized when reviewing a new or existing physical design:

- Is it known which indexes are and are not being used?

- Do all key tables have a clustered index?

- Have the foreign keys been indexed?

- Have the DML effects on each table been considered?

- Is each index's uniqueness strong enough to be useful?

- Is each index's *fillfactor* set properly?

- Is there an index maintenance plan in place?

Unused Indexes

To begin with, it is imperative to know which indexes are not being used for a number of reasons. Indexes take up space, so unused indexes waste storage. Indexes also require maintenance for each DML statement, so there is a performance penalty on tables with many indexes that experience high INSERT, UPDATE and DELETE activity.

With new designs, the DBA may not know what indexes will be used, so the basic standard indexing scheme of primary key indexes, clustered indexes, and indexes on most foreign key columns will need to be performed. If load testing scenarios can be implemented before the first day of production, it could be possible to weed out unused indexes.

So, how can unused indexes be located? The DBA can try the Index Tuning Wizard in SQL Server 7 – 2000 or the Database Tuning Advisor in SQL Server 2005. There are also third party products on the market that will capture and analyze SQL workflow and report on unused indexes. Ambeo is currently one such company.

Clustered Indexes

There is plenty of debate on whether every table should have a clustered index. Many SQL Server gurus suggest that each table should indeed have a clustered index. But, how can one know what series of columns are best suited for a clustered index?

Since clustered indexes sort the underlying table data in the order defined in the index, columns that are the targets of queries that routinely return single or few rows should not be indexed. Instead, a clustered index should be created on one or more columns that are the object of range searches, because the requested data will be found on the same page or pages within close proximity. The end results of smart clustered index designs are reduced I/O and better query response times for queries that return a range of data.

Another benefit of clustered indexes is that they assist in reorganizing a table. Unlike other database engines, SQL Server has no command for reorganizing a heap table. It only works on indexes. So, if there is a badly fragmented table, the DBA is usually stuck with executing a table purge, copying all the data out, truncating the table, and copying all the data back in. This feat is not easy to accomplish in an environment with high amounts of enforced referential integrity.

If the table has a clustered index, the DBA can simply rebuild the clustered index, which reorganizes the data pages because the leaf level of the clustered index is the data.

Foreign Keys

As standard practice, it is wise to index most foreign keys, as they are obvious targets for SQL join operations. Most good modeling tools will automatically generate indexes on all columns involved in referential integrity, so there are few excuses for not having foreign keys indexed properly.

One exception to this is tables that are loaded with foreign keys and the object of intense DML activity, which just so happens to be the the next topic.

Indexes and DML Considerations

When indexing, the DBA must consider the effects of DML activity on the underlying table. If the application is load intensive, meaning that it is primarily one where data is constantly inserted, updated, and deleted, indexing may need to be limited to only the best one-three combination for those tables that bear the brunt of heavy DML work.

In SQL Server 2005, the database can be queried to discover any indexes that appear far out of line with respect to DML activity. The *object_io* query below, shown using the master database as an example, can help pinpoint indexes with heavy leaf page action:

🖫 object_io.sql

```
-- Script is available in the Online Code Depot
```

Indexes and Selectivity

DBAs just stare at some EXPLAIN plans in disbelief because they cannot understand why the optimizer is not using one or more indexes that have been defined on a table. Most database optimizers will not consider an index if the selectivity is low, except for bitmap indexes, which are not available on SQL Server. This being the case, the DBA needs to understand the data distribution of table columns that are being considered for indexing.

The DBCC SHOW_STATISTICS command can help the DBA understand the data distribution of indexes and assist in making smart index choices. If indexes are not used by the optimizer, all that has been achieved is wasted space and potentially worse performance on DML activity.

Indexes and Fillfactor

Some never look at or consider *fillfactor* when creating indexes for a table, which may be just fine in some cases. In other situations, pausing to consider the *fillfactor* effect for indexes is time well spent.

As a quick review, the *fillfactor* effect specifies the percentage of space filled on index data pages when an index is initially created. The default *fillfactor* setting of zero, which can be altered at the global server level through a configuration option, will cause an index to be almost filled to capacity, with only a small amount of space being left at the upper level region of the index. A 100% setting completely fills each index page.

One important thing to remember is that this amount is not adhered to after the index is first built. An index can be rebuilt and the original *fillfactor* setting re-instituted with the variety of DBCC index rebuild or ALTER INDEX (SQL Server 2005) commands.

So, what exactly are the considerations with *fillfactor*? Higher *fillfactor* settings should result in less index pages which in turn should result in fewer pages read during scan operations. As been mentioned many times already, less I/O generally equates to better performance.

However, high *fillfactor* settings can also result in page splits for clustered indexes when SQL Server enforces the sort order of the clustered index

---

during INSERT or UPDATE actions. This happens because SQL Server does not have room on an index page for the requested change, so it has to split the page to perform the modification. This can result in performance degradation and can be confirmed by carefully watching the page splits counter, available from the *page_splits* query below:

🖫 page_splits.sql

```
-- Copyright © 2005 by Rampant TechPress
-- This script is free for non-commercial purposes
-- with no warranties.  Use at your own risk.
--
-- To license this script for a commercial purpose,
-- contact info@rampant.cc
-- ***************************************************

select
    cntr_value
from
    master.dbo.sysperfinfo
where
    counter_name = 'Page Splits/sec' and
    object_name like '%Access methods%'
```

What rules of thumb should be followed with respect to *fillfactor*? If there are tables present that are primarily read only, a *fillfactor* setting of 100 should be used to reduce the number of produced index pages.

If, however, there are tables present with high rates of INSERT, UPDATE and DELETE activity, lower *fillfactor* settings of 50-60% should be used. This will need to be coupled with periodic index rebuilds that will re-establish the *fillfactor* setting to keep DML running smooth through the indexes.

A mixed environment can work well with *fillfactor* settings in the neighborhood of 75%. One last piece of advice: for small indexes that have few pages, time should not be wasted worrying about *fillfactor* as it will not be capable of impacting the database's performance for the worse.

Index Maintenance Plans

To keep indexes in top structural shape, maintenance will be required from time to time. This equates to keeping statistics updated along with periodically reorganizing indexes.

SQL Server is designed to update index statistics automatically through the setting of the AUTO UPDATE STATISTICS option, but many DBAs are not so trusting. The DBA can build a SQL Agent job that executes the *sp_updatestats* procedure. This updates all the statistics in the target database on a schedule that matches the dynamics of the underlying database.

The DBA can also make use of Enterprise Manager/SQL Management Studio's maintenance plan wizard to create a job that updates the statistics of databases. There is more to the maintenance plan wizard than just statistical update functions, so one should take the time and look through what Microsoft offers.

The last time indexes were statistically updated can be checked through use of the *stats_date* function. For example, to see a listing of indexes and the date of their last statistics update, the *last_index_stats* query can be executed:

🖫 last_index_stats

```
-- Copyright © 2005 by Rampant TechPress
-- This script is free for non-commercial purposes
-- with no warranties.  Use at your own risk.
--
-- To license this script for a commercial purpose,
-- contact info@rampant.cc
-- ************************************************

select
    index_name = object_name(id) + '.' + name,
    stat_update_date = stats_date (id,indid),
    indid,
    rows
from
    sysindexes
where
    indid > 1 and
    indid < 255 and
```

```
    name not like '_WA_Sys%'
order by 1
```

One should not be too concerned if a NULL output for the statistics date is seen as the underlying table may have never had any rows in it. These objects can easily be filtered out in the above query by adding a predicate of *and rows > 0*.

Chapter 5 of this book covered how to determine what indexes need to be reorganized, so once again, the chapter should be reviewed for reference material and procedures that provide the diagnostics needed. However, if there are many servers to deal with, it is unlikely time is available to periodically review each database on every server and build reorganization plans on the fly.

The best thing to do is set up smart reorganization jobs that periodically interrogate the active databases and dynamically reorganize only those objects that exceed the predefined thresholds. For example, in SQL Server 2005, this is relatively easy to do; simply execute the *up_index_reorg_2005* procedure below for the databases of interest.

🖫 up_index_reorg_2005

```
-- Script is available in the Online Code Depot
```

The procedure takes a database name as input and uses a predefined threshold of 30% fragmentation which can be overridden.   The procedure should simply be scheduled to run through SQL Agent or a favorite scheduling tool. The index reorganization process can pretty much be set on autopilot.

Smart File and Object Placement

Even with packaged applications, the DBA can improve database performance by intelligently mapping out files and objects at the storage level. This also extends down to what RAID levels are used on the servers.

Storage Structure Planning

While this type of planning generally involves the creation and placement of filegroups and files, one must be careful to not put the cart before the horse. Hardware should be scrutinized first. As was already mentioned above, disk I/O contention must be avoided where possible, so having several disks available to plot out the map of the database is good idea.

At the hardware level, the usual discussion centers on whether to use a redundant array of inexpensive disks (RAID) technology or just a bunch of disks (JBOD). Complicating the decision on what type of RAID to use is that many of the hardware vendors offer smart storage technology that promises to give the DBA the best of both possible worlds.

For example, most DBAs know that write-intensive storage structures should not be placed on a RAID5 setup because of the write penalty that RAID5 imposes. Therefore, the DBA should try to place all transaction logs, TEMPDB databases, and other write-intensive objects on non-RAID5 devices, with the best configuration normally being RAID0+1.

However, a number of hardware vendors claim to have "auto" or "smart" RAID storage devices that offer the protection of RAID5 with the write speed of a RAID0 or RAID1 device. Before going down this route, the DBA should investigate and test the claims of such devices to see if they actually produce the claimed results.

Using Filegroups

SQL Server filegroups allows the DBA to intelligently spread the database among the various disks that exist on the server or SAN. Transaction logs are different in that they do not participate in user defined filegroups; they have their own set of files.

Although DBAs most likely already know how filegroups work, they may wonder if there are any best practice methods that can be employed through filegroups to enhance performance. While every situation is different, there are some rules of thumb that can be utilized when building a database.

When first creating a database, it is good to put all system objects on the *primary* filegroup and separate those from the actual user-defined objects. Putting transaction log files on a separate volume helps lessen the I/O burden on SQL Server, especially if the database will be very write intensive.

Then, create one or more filegroups that exist on volumes that are separate from the initial *primary* and transaction log files. These filegroups will hold the custom database objects. The tables and indexes across separate physical volumes should be further segmented by creating filegroups that hold only tables and indexes.

Tables can be broken down even further by creating filegroups that hold only parts of a table. All versions of SQL Server allow the DBA to place a table's TEXT or IMAGE data on a separate filegroup. Starting in SQL Server 2005, a table can be partitioned across filegroups using the new table partitioning feature. This feature will be covered in more detail later.

If the existing databases are not physically arranged the way desired, the DBA should not despair. New filegroups can be created and objects recreated/rebuilt into those filegroups via standard SQL scripting or through the use of third party SQL Server tools, some of which allow objects to be easily moved between filegroups.

Pinning Tables

While the access times of heavily accessed objects can be improved by placing them in their own filegroups, assuming separate I/O controllers exist for distinct hard drives, the best place for objects to reside will always be memory. With the exception of the large 64 bit servers, current data volumes prohibit placing all objects into RAM. However, the DBA should try to keep all or most of the often-accessed data in memory as the response times will be better than if their data is constantly re-read from disk.

This is accomplished through pinning a table in memory via the DBCC PINTABLE command. A table can also be unpinned through the DBCC UNPINTABLE command. Pinning a table does not toss the pinned object into memory immediately, but as the table is accessed via standard queries, SQL Server will move the table's pages into the buffer cache as it normally would. It will then mark them as pinned, so they will not be flushed as with standard pages.

Small, frequently accessed lookup tables are the best targets for pinning. Large objects should not be considered candidates as their pages could crowd a buffer cache and disallow other objects an otherwise easy entrance into the cache.

Investigate Partitioning

Partitioning is a technique used across all database engines, not just SQL Server. Broadly speaking, partitioning is a method used to physically gather together only certain aspects of the data desired from a particular object. Prior to SQL Server 2005, a partitioning scheme had to be built manually. Whereas, in SQL Server 2005, partitioning is a feature supported through DDL.

There are two primary forms of partitioning: horizontal and vertical.

Horizontal Partitioning

Suppose there is an APPROVAL table in a database containing all doctor approvals for medications given in a hospital. In a very active and dynamic hospital, this type of table can grow exceptionally large. If it is routinely scanned in queries, response times will lengthen in proportion to the number of rows contained in the table.

If the majority of queries target only the current year's data in the APPROVAL table, historical approvals could lie mostly dormant thereby slowing down scans of the table. Such a situation is a good example of when horizontal partitioning will help performance.

Horizontal partitioning splits a table into intelligent data ranges, yet keeps all columns in the table structure in each range. For example, the DBA may have an APPROVAL table that holds the current year's approvals, but then have two other tables, APPROVAL_2004 and APPROVAL_2005, that hold approvals for prior years. Figure 10.5 is a representation of horizontal partitioning.

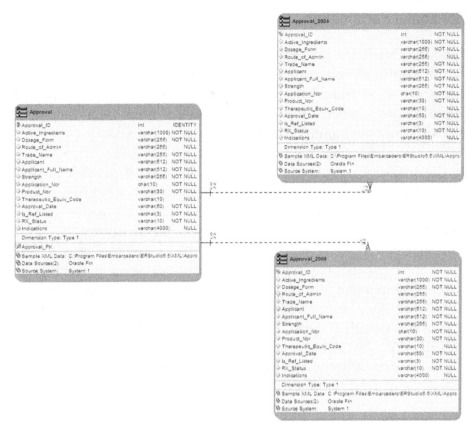

Figure 10.5: *Horizontally partitioning a table.*

By using this technique, the amount of data held in the table most often accessed by user activities can be greatly reduced. This improves query response times while retaining historical data for future availability.

If user queries need to reference the approvals for all years, a view called *approve_all,* composed of a union of all horizontally partitioned tables, can be created.

Vertical Partitioning

Vertical partitioning is not as common as horizontal, but it is still used in some cases. Since rows in SQL Server cannot span across multiple pages, the number of rows per page is very much determined by the width of the table itself.

Vertical partitioning is a way to reduce the width of a table by splitting it into two or more tables that contain a subset of the originating table's columns. The idea is that the reduced width tables will be able to store more rows per data page. Therefore, I/O will be reduced during scan operations because more data can be read per page. Figure 10.6 is a representation of vertical partitioning.

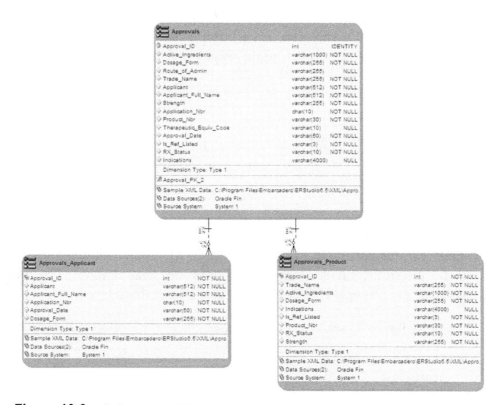

Figure 10.6: *Splitting a table vertically.*

For vertical partitioning to work, queries must exist that require only a subset of columns from the original table.

Partitioning in SQL Server 2005

Microsoft has finally introduced support for partitioning through DDL in SQL Server 2005. This capability has been offered by Oracle since version 8.0. DDL partitioning allows a table to be logically subdivided into horizontal sections while keeping all partitions under the same table umbrella.

SQL Server differs from Oracle in that the partitioning scheme is defined outside of the actual table DDL. For example, a health care administrator decides to subdivide a hospital's admissions by year. In SQL Server 2005, this can be accomplished by defining a partition *function*, which defines the partition ranges as follows:

```
CREATE PARTITION FUNCTION AdmissionDateRange(datetime)
AS
RANGE LEFT FOR VALUES (
    '19990101 23:59:59.997',
    '20000101 23:59:59.997',
    '20010101 23:59:59.997',
    '20020101 23:59:59.997',
    '20030101 23:59:59.997',
    '20040101 23:59:59.997',
    '20050101 23:59:59.997')
```

The next step is to create a partition *scheme*. This permits the DBA to direct various partitions to certain physical filegroups, allowing the table to be physically divided among different physical devices. This helps alleviate any physical I/O contention at the hard drive level:

```
CREATE PARTITION SCHEME AdmissionDateScheme
AS
PARTITION AdmissionDateRange
TO ([FG1],
    [FG2],
    [FG3],
    [FG4],
    [FG5],
    [FG6],
    [FG7],
    [FG8])
```

In the absence of multiple disks on which to spread the table partitions, all can be placed on one filegroup by way of the following statement:

```
CREATE PARTITION SCHEME AdmissionDateScheme
AS
PARTITION AdmissionDateRange
ALL TO ([FG1])
```

Once a partition function and scheme is defined, a partitioned table can be created as in the following example:

```
CREATE TABLE dbo.ADMISSION_PARTITIONED
(
    ADMISSION_ID      numeric(19,0) NOT NULL,
    ADMISSION_TIME    datetime      NOT NULL,
    RELEASE_TIME      datetime      NULL,
    RELEASE_COMMENTS  varchar(250)  NULL,
    NURSE_ID          numeric(19,0) NOT NULL,
    PATIENT_ID        numeric(19,0) NOT NULL
)
ON AdmissionDateScheme (ADMISSION_TIME)
```

Indexes can then be created on the partitioned table that are partitioned either locally, the same as each underlying partition, or globally.

As with manual partitioning in SQL Server 7 and 2000, the goal is to intelligently subdivide a table into segments that are logically accessed together. Scans and other functions that make use of the partition function would only scan the needed partitions instead of the entire table. The end result being less I/O and improved response times.

Partitioning through Data Archiving

Data archiving should be thought of as horizontal partitioning for an entire application or system. The concept of data archiving is especially prevalent in the world of packaged financial applications where a database's object count is in the thousands and small subsystems of related information are present.

In these situations, the DBA cannot just begin taking single tables and splitting them horizontally due to the complexity of the underlying database design and myriads of referential integrity definitions. Instead, a methodology of splitting either the entire application horizontally or intelligently splitting the various sub-designs that make up the application is needed.

While on a more grand scale, the basic goal is still the same: move seldom accessed or historical data to structures that may still be referenced and leave in place the current or most needed data in the primary data structures. With less data on the primary system, scans and other I/O functions should complete much faster.

With data archiving, it is common to move the historical data to a database outside the primary server so internal resources can labor on data needed the most. The data from the primary database can be linked to the archived data through traditional methods used to pull data from other servers, linked servers and etc. Some data archiving software includes middleware to assist in the access of archived data.

In addition to periodically moving data, data archiving software also assists in the elimination of outdated information. Purge routines can be set up on the archived database to periodically remove data that has outlived its usefulness.

Data archiving for large systems is not something normally tackled through custom, in-house processes. It is accomplished through sophisticated software that understands today's most common financial packages such as Peoplesoft, now owned by Oracle, and Oracle Financials.

Some archiving software also provides methods for archiving data from custom database applications. A DBA chooses a subset of tables to archive and selects a driving table along with conditions on when to move data. At this point the archiving software takes over.

Denormalization Techniques

Data modeling purists tend to look down on denormalizing a logical design. However, for performance reasons, it is often necessary at the

---

physical design level. The concepts of normalization, which is the removal of repeating groups and attributes depending on a primary key, etc., will not be covered in this book as these fundamental concepts should be well known to any database architect. Instead, techniques will be studied that can be applied to certain situations in a logical design that will help performance at the physical database stage.

Benefits of Good Normalization

Relational database normalization has a number of performance-related benefits besides the standard reasons database architects utilize the practice. Before a database is denormalized, the potential benefits must be weighed against the following:

- Normalization guards against the storage of redundant data, and therefore helps reduce DML I/O because a piece of information is stored and modified in only one place.

- Wide tables are often avoided because columns in a table are only present when they depend on the primary key of the table. Narrower tables result in more rows being stored on a physical SQL Server page; therefore, they can result in less I/O during scan operations as fewer pages need to be read.

- Use of composite indexes tends to be reduced. Wide indexes, like wide tables, can result in more pages being read during index scan requests than single column indexes.

Recognizing Denormalization Candidates

How does one know when to apply denormalization to a particular database? While every case is different, the following list includes some common indicators:

- Any amount of meaningful data, information that can be read and understood by application users, can only be obtained through joining four or more tables together.

- Data that is frequently the target of query search arguments must be computed by combining two or more columns.

- Data is routinely requested in aggregate forms rather than in the singular nature in which it is stored.

- Subsets of data (for example, by date range) are ordinarily requested, rather than the entire volume of data stored for a particular object or set of objects.

- Column subsets in a table are often requested with other columns being completely neglected by application queries.

The last two points in the above list are typically addressed through partitioning. The others are handled through storing redundant data, storing computed values, and pre-building aggregated data structures.

Storing Redundant Data

Storing redundant data is by far the most common denormalization technique. As the DBA surveys common resource-intensive queries, it will be seen that tables are commonly used over and over again.

Initial targets of this form of denormalization are lookup tables that contain nothing more than a numeric primary key and a character description of the lookup entity. For example, a lookup table might contain a list of medication names that are unique in order to ensure that no medication name is duplicated. By removing the table and substituting the medication name in any table that references it, the DBA has removed at least one join from the queries requiring that information.

Consideration here should be given to the updates of the medication name. If the names change often, the application must be altered to update every table containing the medication name, rather than just updating it in one place.

Supertypes and subtype entities are other common targets for denormalization. For example, in an HR application, an employee entity that stores common information for all employees may exist. This is known as a supertype entity. The HR application may have different forms of employees, each with their own specific attributes. For instance, sales employees and managers each have data that needs to be stored only as it relates to them. These are called subtypes because they descend, as it were, from the supertype employee entity. Figure 10.7 illustrates the super and subtypes used in denormalization.

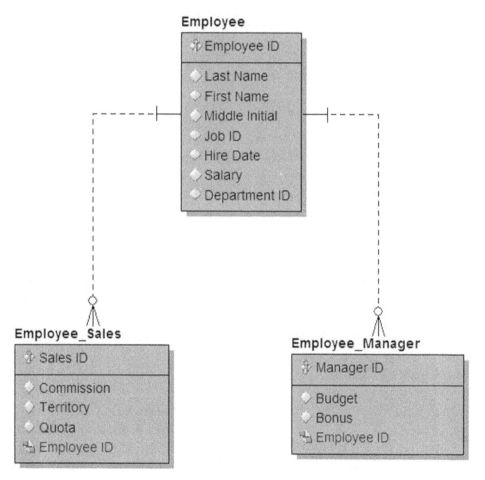

Figure 10.7: *Super and sub types make good denormalization candidates.*

By combining a supertype with all its subtypes, the DBA can reduce join queries that require base employee information and specific data as it relates to a particular employee type, such as sales.

Computed or Virtual Columns

If a query routinely searches on computed values between two columns, the DBA may benefit from using a virtual column in SQL Server. Note the following query:

```
select
    emp_id
from
    employee
where
    salary + commission > 100000
```

Performance can be aided by the creation of a computed column in the table called TOTAL_COMP in the following fashion:

```
create table employee
(emp_id            int,
 salary            decimal(10,2),
 commission decimal(10,2),
 total_comp as (salary + commission))
```

The actual data is not stored in SQL Server, but it is maintained internally in SQL Server 7-2000. There is an option of storing the data in SQL Server 2005. These columns can also be indexed in SQL Server 2000 and higher.

Aggregated Data

Database performance can be greatly improved when a DBA creates summary tables that contain aggregated information from detail objects in the database. While this need is often seen in data warehouses, it is becoming just as common in standard OLTP applications as almost every application has business intelligence needs these days.

SQL Server does not offer the flexibility of Oracle or DB2 in building objects to help in this area. Oracle offers materialized views, and DB2 has summary tables. SQL Server does provide indexed views, but there is a laundry list of requirements and no options for providing flexibility when the summarized data is refreshed from the underlying detail objects.

Whether a DBA opts for the indexed view or builds customized objects, the performance improvements in queries that access such aggregate objects over their detailed counterparts can be dramatic.

Storing Only Changed Data

One technique that helps cut down on the amount of detail data stored in a database involves storing information only when a change is detected. Such a method can drastically reduce the amount of data piled into a database, regardless of the database application.

For example, if there is an application that monitors the outside temperature every five minutes, the data inserted into a table may appear as follows:

```
01/01/2005 07:00    70
01/01/2005 07:05    70
01/01/2005 07:10    70
01/01/2005 07:15    70
01/01/2005 07:20    70
01/01/2005 07:25    71
01/01/2005 07:30    71
01/01/2005 07:35    71
01/01/2005 07:40    71
01/01/2005 07:45    71
```

Instead of inputting data every five minutes, one may choose to insert data only when a change is detected. In the above examples, only two rows would be inserted instead of ten, significantly reducing the amount of data entered.

Such a technique may mean an additional burden is placed upon the application in terms of computational requirements. But employing such a technique is usually worth the extra effort, since quite a bit of physical I/O is eliminated at the database level.

Conclusion

The tuning stage in Performance Lifecycle Management involves taking action based on the diagnostic findings uncovered through proactive performance testing, intelligent monitoring, trend analysis, and forecasting. This should not be mistaken for the end of the road. The cycle of testing, analysis and tuning will be repeated many times before the database is running at optimum efficiency.

Although every case is different, SQL Server, for the most part, is tuned through configuration changes, optimizing resource-intensive SQL, and altering the physical database design. Once the right data is obtained, making configuration changes is not too difficult.

The same cannot be said, however, for optimizing SQL and the underlying database design. These two tasks generally require a more intimate knowledge of SQL Server operation. Attention has been focused on those areas that help SQL Server run as efficiently as possible.

By adhering to each step in the Performance Lifecycle, the high performance SQL Server DBA will be able to squeeze every last drop of performance out of Microsoft's database engine, and experience much more success than those who use a haphazard approach to performance management. As with most things, organization and discipline will win out over blind chance every time.

Index

About the Author

Robin Schumacher is Vice-President of Product Management for Embarcadero Technologies, Inc., a leading supplier of database software tools. Robin has over fourteen years experience in database administration, development, monitoring, and tuning with Oracle, DB2, Teradata, Sybase, and Microsoft SQL Server.

He has authored countless performance-related articles for many database-centric magazines as well as serving as a database software reviewer and feature writer for the likes of Intelligent Enterprise, eWeek, DM Review, and others.

About Mike Reed

When he first started drawing, Mike Reed drew just to amuse himself. It wasn't long, though, before he knew he wanted to be an artist. Today he does illustrations for children's books, magazines, catalogs, and ads.

He also teaches illustration at the College of Visual Art in St. Paul, Minnesota. Mike Reed says, "Making pictures is like acting — you can paint yourself into the action." He often paints on the computer, but he also draws in pen and ink and paints in acrylics. He feels that learning to draw well is the key to being a successful artist.

Mike is regarded as one of the nation's premier illustrators and is the creator of the popular "Flame Warriors" illustrations at www.flamewarriors.com, a website devoted to Internet insults. "To enter his Flame Warriors site is sort of like entering a hellish Sesame Street populated by Oscar the Grouch and 83 of his relatives." – Los Angeles Times.
(http://redwing.hutman.net/%7Emreed/warriorshtm/lat.htm)

Mike Reed has always enjoyed reading. As a young child, he liked the Dr. Seuss books. Later, he started reading biographies and war stories. One reason why he feels lucky to be an illustrator is because he can listen to books on tape while he works. Mike is available to provide custom illustrations for all manner of publications at reasonable prices. Mike can be reached at www.mikereedillustration.com.